DEDICATION

To my mother, Florence Sexter Magezis, a woman of wisdom and inner strength who planted and nourished the seeds of creative possibilities which flowered into this book.

ACKNOWLEDGEMENTS

I would like to thank the many women who read over sections of this book and contributed their helpful comments and suggestions. They are Rahelly Cutting Ben Meir, Sue Ulrich, Adarsh Grewal, Marilyn Jones, Kathy Leander, Mary Feeney, Jill Hooker, Val Richards, Sheila Robin, Sonya McKay, Louise Gilchrist and Doreen Dace. Thanks to the Cambridge Women's Writers (Sally Cline, Chris Carling, Marion Callen and Geraldine Ryan) for their support and suggestions and the Cambridge Women's Resources Centre for the loan of their books.

My family was of great help to me during the process of writing this book. I would like to thank Martin Magezis, Susan Berkowitz, Fannie and Ed Biderman, Ruth and Jerry Sobin, Kerin Biderman, Kevin Biderman and most especially Bob Biderman.

I would like to thank my editor, Lucy Purkis, for suggesting the idea for this book and for her help. And I would like to thank Sophie Grillet for her wonderful cartoons.

CONTENTS

1
LOOKING AT
WOMEN'S STUDIES

Women's studies is like a beautiful sculpture, made by women. As you walk round it, you see such different sides. Soon you discover it's unfinished, awaiting your additions.

What is women's studies?

Women's studies is putting women centre-stage. For too long women were the 'also' of 'mankind'. But things are changing, though many more changes are needed, and women's studies is helping to make them happen. It's about giving women a fair chance to live up to their potential. Women's studies brings together our personal experiences and the study of ideas. It is a way of examining the world from women's points of view, coming to understand it and then making changes. Into the twenty-first century, we women need to take hold of our future.

What can you gain from women's studies?

Women's studies can help us build the confidence to take ourselves seriously. We look at the forces around us, the social factors which mould us, like how we were treated as girls. We can explore how we have been shaped by being women and the ways in which we've been hindered from reaching our potential. Women's studies also takes into account the other factors which affect us like our race, ethnic background, class, sexuality, age and level of ability.

Understanding is the first step in having some control of the social forces around us. The process of thinking things out and gaining knowledge about ourselves and other women can help us to have power over our lives.

Looking at the many accomplishments of women can enable us to believe in our own abilities. As we learn about women's lives in the past, their courage, their problems and their victories, we can see our own lives more clearly.

Women's studies can also put us in contact with other women, through courses and networking. Our strength in working together and exploring ideas helps us all move forward.

Where did women's studies come from?

In the late 1960s women who had been working for the rights of others began to question their own treatment. We took the vision we had of working for justice and turned it round towards ourselves. We were shocked to see that we were ending up making the tea and not being taken seriously. So we began meeting by ourselves, in Consciousness Raising Groups, talking about the common ways we'd been kept down as women.

The talk led to action. Women from the US and Canada demonstrated outside the Miss America Beauty Contest in 1968. They used street theatre to show how women were being **oppressed** (in the sense of being kept down through an unjust exercise of power) by having to compete for, and live up to, an idealised male image of what they should be like. Later British women demonstrated at the Miss World Beauty Contest.

There was also an upsurge of women asserting their rights in employment. In 1968 a strike by women at the Ford Motor plant in Dagenham, near London led to the promise of equal pay legislation. The following year there was a large demonstration by women for equal pay in Trafalgar Square, London. Other strikes and demonstrations followed as women's campaigning groups increased. In more and more countries, women began meeting together in various industries, trade unions, organisations and universities.

As the Women's Liberation Movement started to blossom, women students (having been through student revolts concerning student rights, civil rights, demands for Ethnic Studies courses and anti-Vietnam War activities) began demanding courses on women. They also demanded changes in other academic subjects to take on board women's perspectives.

One of the fruits of the Women's Liberation Movement was women's studies. But like a new plant, it developed into something more. Growing (and it's still fairly young) in the soil of higher, further and adult education has meant, on one hand, creating academic language and theory as well as following certain rules. On the other hand, women's studies has worked to change education and has tried to keep women's experiences as part of what we study.

EXERCISE 1.1 **Your views**

Examine your own views

1 What does it mean to you to be a woman?
2 What do you have in common with other women?

Express your views

1 Keep a journal of your thoughts and feelings while reading this book, or even tape record them.
2 Use any creative medium which you feel comfortable with, such as art, music or creative writing, to respond to the ideas in this book.

What does it mean to be a woman?

For me, what it means to be a woman involves nurturing, wanting to take care of others and being loved for it by them. I also relate being a woman to a kind of sensitivity to emotions and being able to talk out problems. Then again, I have a strong sense of defiance against being pigeon-holed or stereotyped because I'm a woman.

Your answer may have been very different than mine. There's no right or wrong answer. So where does our sense of being a woman come from? Is it **biological** (i.e. what we were born with from our genes) or does it come from our **culture** (the values, experiences and beliefs we share with others)?

Sex and gender

In trying to answer the question of what is biological and what is cultural about being a woman, Ann Oakley, a feminist sociologist and writer, explored the distinction between sex and gender. By **sex** we mean everything which is biological about being a woman. This would include being able to reproduce (whether or not we can or want to have children), our female genes, our sex organs and our hormones. By **gender** we mean those things which are expected of a woman by her culture. For example, women being seen as more able to talk about their feelings. Looking at it this way, what is 'feminine' or 'masculine' has been built up by our society, rather than being born within us. We can see this clearly when we examine the differences in the way girls and boys are raised. The toys they are given show gender expectations for their future. Girls are more likely to be given baby dolls or dress up fashion dolls, while boys usually get cars, sports equipment and computer games.

In any given country, female gender expectations are what is now considered feminine there. But even within the same country, there are many different ideas of what it means to be feminine. To see this we only have to look at styles of dress of teenage girls and older women. Not only does femininity mean different things to different groups of people in the same culture, it also varies in different cultures.

Gender expectations change over time. For example, since the

Women's Liberation Movement began in the late 1960s there have been some changes. So what it means to be a woman, or a man for that matter, can and does change.

It's important to see that we can change society's gender expectations and those expectations which are inside oneself that is, **internalised**. This potential for change allows us to think of many possibilities for more equal treatment of ourselves and other women. Changing gender differences can also be helpful for men who, for example, often feel boxed-in by not being able to cry or express their emotions.

EXERCISE 1.2 **Think of your own life**

1 How were you moulded by your gender?
2 How are you being limited by what is expected of you as a woman?
3 What kinds of possibilities can you imagine for yourself based on changes in gender expectations?

Earlier, I mentioned personally linking nurturing with being a woman. Are my nurturing feelings 100 per cent gender based? Do I feel nurturing simply because in our culture people expect women to want to take care of others? Well, nothing is that simple, is it? And there's a growing feeling in Women's Studies that there isn't always a clear-cut line between sex and gender. For me, my nurturing feelings increased after having children, but even this must have been influenced by the expectations of others. Although nurturing has a strong basis in gender, I would hope it was also a human quality. In any case, since nurturing is so useful to our society, why is it not more highly valued economically? Why are attributes which are seen as belonging to the female gender undervalued in our society?

Clearly, there is a relationship between gender and power. In a general sense, **power** is being able to produce an effect. That effect could be economic or political, but it could also be psychological or cultural. Later in the chapter we will see how different feminists view the subject of power. Throughout this book we will look at the issue of power from different angles, as one important aim of Women's Studies is to help us gain more power.

Looking at our differences

While it's easier to see what's biological about being a woman, when it comes to cultural expectations, we find we're not only affected by being female. Expectations have been placed on us, based on the ways in which we are different from the dominant culture in society. These differences include our class, race, ethnic background, sexuality, age and level of ability. Just as with the issue of gender, we find our differences are used to keep us from gaining power over our lives.

As women we can find ourselves being stereotyped. **Stereotyping** is seeing a person in an oversimplified, one-sided way, not based on their individuality but based on pre-judging them because they are a member of a particular group. For example, a stereotypical expectation of women is that they won't be able to be skilled in technology. Similarly, women who are in some way different from the dominant culture in society (such as Black, lesbian and/or disabled women) can find themselves burdened with additional stereotypes.

Understanding our differences can help us to respect each other and celebrate our diversity, which will enrich us all. This understanding can bring us closer together and can also assist us, individually, in freeing ourselves of our internalised cultural expectations.

Our differences can not be divided off from the issue of being a woman, because they are part of our identity. Our unique **identity** is a combination of all the elements of who we are. By looking at our individual identity from a number of different angles, we can gain a clearer picture of ourselves and how we have been affected by various cultural expectations.

EXERCISE 1.3 **Looking at our differences**

1 In what ways are you different than other women?
2 How would you set out these differences?
3 Which is the most important to you and why?

Race and ethnicity

Here is what Alice Walker had to say about Black women in her book, *In Search of our Mothers' Gardens.*

Black women are called, in the folklore that so aptly identifies one's status in society, "the *mule* of the world", because we have been handed the burdens that everyone else – *everyone* else – refused to carry. We have also been called "Matriarchs," "Superwomen," and "Mean and Evil Bitches." Not to mention "Castraters" and "Sapphire's Mama." When we have pleaded for understanding, our character has been distorted; when we have asked for simple caring, we have been handed empty inspirational appellations, then stuck in the farthest corner. When we have asked for love, we have been given children. In short, even our plainer gifts, our labors of fidelity and love, have been knocked down our throats. To be an artist and a black woman, even today, lowers our status in many respects, rather than raises it: and yet, artists we will be.

Differences in race and ethnicity have often been used to keep us apart, to set up an 'us' and 'them' situation. This has been used for economic and political control. Just as women have faced **discrimination** (i.e. have not been given an equal chance, based on stereotyping), people who are not part of the dominant race and/or ethnic group within a society have often been kept from full participation.

There can be problems in using the term 'race' because too often it has been used to justify the superiority of one race over another by pointing to biological differences between people. In fact, as UNESCO points out, all human beings come from the same species; biological differences between them are minor and do not affect their innate mental characteristics or their social and cultural development. I use the word 'race' throughout this book in order to discuss **racism** (i.e. discrimination based on the false notion of racial superiority).

The idea of racial superiority, which has no basis in scientific fact, was used as an excuse for slavery. It has been used by colonial powers to control people and treat them inhumanely. Most developing nations have struggled to gain their independence from colonising countries.

In the 1960s the US Civil Rights Movement served as an inspiring example of how the notion of racial superiority, and the political and economic power behind it, can be exposed and challenged. Today, although there are movements in many countries against racism, this same false notion of racial superiority is still used as an excuse to keep people from gaining power over their lives.

It is important to point out that the term 'Black' is used differently in Britain than in some countries such as the United States. As Amina Mama (a Nigerian-born feminist activist and writer in Britain) explains, in the US, Black refers only to those people of African descent and the term 'women of color' is used in a more general sense to include others such as Hispanic and Native American women. In Britain, the term 'Black' is used in a political sense to refer to both Asians (primarily from the Indian subcontinent) and Africans and their **descendants** (that is, those of future generations who may have moved to other parts of the world). This is a complex issue as women define their identity for themselves. Throughout this book I use the term 'Black' in a political sense.

The term **ethnic group** refers to people who share a common culture. For me the biggest difference I feel as a woman is being Jewish. I remember being at a Jewish feminist conference in Manchester, involved in a small group discussion with other women who had all been born in Britain. Although they certainly considered themselves British, as we talked it came out that on a deep, inner level all of them felt themselves to be foreigners because they were Jewish.

It was reading Rosario Morales's piece, 'I am what I am', that made that sense of being foreign clearer for me. In it she talks about the sweet Yiddish words which have made their way into American English. For me Yiddish is the mother tongue which I barely know, though its way of thinking is so much a part of my consciousness, just as its gestures and way of talking are part of my speech. Yet in Britain I work at holding them back to fit in. I try not to use 'my foreign Yiddish words' which others won't understand or else I use them consciously and defiantly. Perhaps that's why I sometimes feel 'more myself' in places which have an ethnic/racial mix like Kilburn, in London, where everyone can be who they are. But ethnic difference is more than just a question of language. For example, because Irish women in Britain have been viewed as inferior outsiders they have experienced discrimination.

As we look at the values and the expectations of the society around us, we begin to see how much we've been influenced by them. Women's studies looks at these influences to help us see if we too have stereotyped expectations of others based, for example, on their race or ethnic background. Finding stereotyped expectations within ourselves may be painful, but it can also be a freeing process as we take responsibility for changing the way we think about our experiences.

Class

A working-class friend of mine, who was looking for a job, told me about a possible opening that she felt she couldn't apply for. She explained, 'It's not my place. They all have posh accents there.' Discussing this led us to talking about class expectations and the barriers we have to overcome.

Of course, women are not primarily being held back by their own internalised class expectations, but, more significantly, by those of society. Gender expectations have been used as an excuse for lower pay for all women, but working-class women are hit hardest. While as a whole in employment there is a difference between the pay of men and women, the **salary gender gap**, amongst women, working-class women tend to have the low-status, low-paying jobs.

There are economic divisions between women which mean that some of us have been given more privileges than others. Economic power plays an important role in our society and women find themselves in different relationships to it. This not only affects the income of working-class women, but their treatment both in employment and in the society as a whole. For example, society's stereotyped educational expectations of working-class women has limited their educational achievements.

Working-class women have played a primary role in organising for their rights, such as earlier this century in the garment industry in the US and in Britain in strikes such as the Grunwick's Strike in London in the 1970s. They have also played a leading role in movements to save their communities, for example, in the 1984/85 Miners' Strike in Britain. But working-class women have only recently begun to gain the recognition they deserve both in trade unions and political organisations and in the women's movement as a whole.

Sexual identity

In the past, and even still today, women have felt they had to hide their lesbian relationships for fear of being physically attacked, losing

[handwritten marginal note: Economic differences (sciences)]

their jobs, their homes and even their children.

When the Women's Liberation Movement began to blossom, the Gay Liberation Movement was also taking shape. Lesbians and gay men began to 'come out' and campaign for their equal rights, which still have not been completely achieved. Some lesbians involved with the Women's Liberation Movement felt they needed to look at both women's issues and issues of homosexuality and formed lesbian organisations and support networks. As time went on, ideas about women controlling and choosing their sexual identity were increasingly discussed in the Women's Liberation Movement, which began demanding an end to discrimination against lesbians.

Looking at society's expectations of women, we can see that those women who choose to have relationships with other women have been stereotyped as strange creatures who should be feared for giving up their 'femininity' to act in what is perceived as a threateningly 'masculine' way. But 'masculinity' and 'femininity' are created by society. In reality lesbians look and act in many different ways, have a wide spectrum of opinions and play an assortment of different roles in our society, including being mothers.

The lesbian feminist writer Adrienne Rich is critical of society's expectations. In *Blood, Bread and Poetry* she points out that, 'Lesbian existence is also represented as mere refuge from male abuses, rather than as an electric and empowering charge between women.'

Level of ability

Here is how Mary Greaves, MBE, MA, BSc, described the effect on females of becoming disabled in her preface to *Better Lives for Disabled Women*.

> I was just an ordinary little girl with fair curly hair wearing pretty dresses made by my mother until suddenly, one day in November when I was three-and-a-half years old I ceased being a little girl and became a 'polio'. Just a few hours and I was 'neutered' – a sexless little creature.
>
> My hair was cut like a boy's (in those days boys didn't have long hair and girls didn't have short hair). I wore boy's jerseys over a nightdress until I was about eight years old. But I wasn't a little boy. One eminent consultant greeted me in those early days

with, 'Now, my little man and how are you today?' To which I answered scornfully, 'Mary is a girl's name.' This little incident illustrates what I am sure a great many disabled girls and women feel – they are deprived of their femininity, and in consequence their role as a woman, because of their disability.'

Sisters Against Disablement point out that they are disabled by society. Women who are especially challenged have been particularly injured by the fantasy image of a perfect female body and by narrow, destructive boundaries set on what it means to be 'normal'.

The term 'Temporarily Able-bodied' has been used to show that disabilities are set up by society's expectations and that each of us will change our level of abilities over the course of our lives. **Accessibility** (in the sense of being able to come into a place or situation) is something we need to create for everyone.

In *Mustn't Grumble*, Lois Keith points out that by talking with other women with disabilities she came to see that it was not her fault that she could not fully participate, but was because the laws and regulations of society had been designed to shut out people with disabilities. In this book women with disabilities define their own lives, beyond the mythology of female disability, honestly discussing the complexity of their existence – involving pain and struggle for their rights, but also warmth, humour and accomplishment.

A ring of fear and suspicion has been created around women who are especially challenged, including those with special mental health needs. To melt that icy ring we must each examine our own expectations of 'disabilities'. This process can help us come to terms with our own fears about our physical and mental state. Accepting each woman for who she is can bring us closer together so that we can all work to remove society's barriers.

Age

Older Women's Liberation, which included consciousness raising groups, campaigning groups and networks, was a part of the Women's Liberation Movement. It focused on everything from health to heating and from pensions to stereotypes of older women.

Stereotypes of older women being helpless and useless deny the reality of their lives. Older women have been seen to be no longer necessary because of society's expectation that their only value was in taking care of children. After the menopause women have often been made invisible by the media or misrepresented as lacking in sexuality. The reality is that older women play all kinds of useful roles from doctors to community leaders and from artists to university professors. In *The Fountain of Age*, Betty Friedan suggests that one reason women live longer than men is because of their flexibility in playing different roles and their ability to adapt to change.

In the book *Growing Old Disgracefully*, older women publicly bring to light taboo subjects concerning themselves. Recently the taboo subject of menopause has been more publicly discussed, for example, in Germaine Greer's book *The Change*. Menopause Support Groups have been formed as a way for women to help define their own experiences and their own futures.

The fullness of our identity

Our identity is a rich tapestry with many different elements woven together. In this way women may fit into more than one category of difference and may define themselves in many different ways. Here is what Audre Lorde had to say about her own life and the issue of difference in 1980 in *Sister Outsider*.

> As a forty-nine-year-old Black lesbian feminist socialist mother of two, including one boy, and a member of an interracial couple, I usually find myself a part of some group defined as other, deviant, inferior, or just plain wrong....

> Institutionalised rejection of difference is an absolute necessity in a profit economy which needs outsiders as surplus people. As members of such an economy, we have *all* been programmed to respond to human differences between us with fear and loathing... Certainly there are very real differences between us of race, age and sex. But it is not these differences between us that are separating us. It is rather our refusal to recognise those differences, and to examine the distortions which result from our misnaming them and their effects upon human behaviour and expectation.

EXERCISE 1.4 **Look at your own expectations**

(Honestly recognising your own stereotyped expectations is the first step toward changing them.)

1 In what ways have you internalised stereotyped expectations about yourself?
2 How has this limited you?
3 What stereotyped expectations do you have toward other women?

What is feminism?

Feminism is based on the idea that society is not treating women fairly. It looks at why this is so and how women are oppressed. It works for women's liberation.

The definition I've just given is a very general one. Whole books have been written, trying to say what feminism is. In *What is Feminism?*, edited by Juliet Mitchell and Ann Oakley, women look at the question from different angles. The point is that feminism means different things to different women. For example, some would say it is working for equality with men in our society, while others say it is out to change the whole way society is set up.

Feminism is a broad social movement which allows different points of views under the umbrella of working for women's rights and against female oppression. Whether or not you want to call yourself a feminist is something that only you can decide. But don't feel that you have to use the title in order to find out about women's studies.

Different feminist points of view

Below I have listed the main feminist points of view. It is useful to examine them to see how different kinds of feminists look at the causes of women's oppression, what can be done to free them and the issue of power in society. But that doesn't mean that every feminist has to fit into one of these categories. Some women feel that in the 1990s there has been a knitting together of the various view points.

Socialist feminists

Socialist feminists see oppression by gender, class and race as three strong vines which have become so intertwined that they can no longer be separated. These vines have grown into an enormous branch, which holds women down. All the vines must be cut to free women.

Women's oppression is based both on male dominance and economic inequality, they believe. Socialist feminists not only view all women as oppressed because of their gender, but also see some women as oppressed because of their race, ethnicity, class, sexual identity, age and/or level of ability. These women will have the same interests as men in these groups. Therefore, socialist feminists view every form of oppression as a women's issue, about which women may either want to organise separately or join with men.

Although they see the need for women's groups, female-only centres and women's **caucuses** (groupings within larger organisations to look out for special interests), they feel feminists should also join with other social movements working for justice. The socialist feminist writers Sheila Rowbotham, Lynne Segal and Hilary Wainwright talked about bringing feminism and socialism together in a new way in the book *Beyond the Fragments*.

'Socialist Feminist' is a general term which takes in a number of different kinds of feminists who consider themselves socialists. These include Marxist feminists, humanist feminists, and unaligned socialist feminists.

Radical feminists

Radical feminists believe that women's oppression is caused by patriarchy. **Patriarchy** is the social, political and economic system of male power over women. They see society as controlled by male rulers who use women and benefit from their reproductive capacity. This is done by treating women as inferior and gaining at their expense.

As well as seeing an overall male military, industrial, religious and political rule, radical feminists believe that individual men have power over women and children through the family. Viewing basic differences in power between men and women, they divide the world into male and female, thus seeing women's oppression as the most important kind. Therefore, radical feminists believe that for women to take control of their lives, they must separate themselves and their interests from the influence of men.

Radical feminists work to create women-only centres, organisations, institutions and businesses. Questioning values developed under patriarchy, they've created the idea of women focusing on their own experiences and setting their own values – **woman-centredness**. This includes seeing the positive sides of previously undervalued feminine qualities. Adrienne Rich and Mary Daly each wrote about what they felt these female qualities were.

Revolutionary feminists
Revolutionary feminism came out of radical feminism. Although they both see men, as a group, being the cause of women's oppression, revolutionary feminism takes the idea of radical feminism one step further campaigning to make a revolution against men's power over women and calling for total separation. In Britain in 1981, the Leeds Revolutionary Feminists published a pamphlet in which they called for the main focus of campaigning to be on male violence against women.

Psychoanalytic feminists

Psychoanalytic feminists use Freud's main idea of the unconscious to understand and challenge women's oppression, while rejecting his view of '**penis envy**' (that women supposedly feel lacking because of their biology). The **unconscious** is that part of the mind which you don't have direct access to. For example, the unconscious comes out in dreams and is often indirectly and unintentionally drawn upon when thinking, talking or making decisions.

Psychoanalytic feminists believe that the idea of the unconscious is useful in explaining how power relationships between men and women are formed, how they are internalised and how they can be changed. They see patriarchy existing not only in society but within ourselves; our identity is formed not just by what we are conscious of, but by the unconscious. They believe it is important in the process of change to take into account the unconscious.

In writing *Psychoanalysis and Feminism* in 1974, Juliet Mitchell became one of the first feminists to argue that although Freud's ideas had been used to justify patriarchy, women should turn them into a tool to analyse patriarchy. She felt that capitalism and patriarchy had become interlocked in such a way that socialism alone would not free women. They needed to understand how deeply they had internalised patriarchal values in order to have the means to unlock the unconscious processes which kept these values in place.

Melanie Klein, who was active earlier this century, around the same time as Freud, started the Object Relations School. She especially focused on infancy and the early relationship between mother and baby. Present day feminists have built on her theories. For example, Luise Eichenbaum and Susie Orbach have studied the relationship between mothers and daughters.

Some recent psychoanalytic work has focused on issues of difference. This includes work on the experience of racism, cultural difference, disability and hatred or fear of lesbians or gay men – **homophobia**.

Black feminists

Black feminists believe that Black women must define their own views and their own identity, rather than leaving this to white women or Black men. At times this has put them in the difficult position of having to criticise both white feminists and Black men. Although the Women's Liberation Movement of the late 1960s and 1970s wished to speak for all women, it was basically white and middle class. Thus, in a number of important ways, it did not reflect or appreciate the experiences of Black and/or working-class women.

Black feminist ideas come out of the experiences of ordinary Black women. They are based on the principle that racism and sexism are cemented together and that they should not be separated or pitted against each other. The US-based Combahee River Collective pointed out the need to work with Black men against racism while still struggling with them about sexism. They felt that both patriarchy and the political-economic system had to be destroyed for them to be free. bell hooks argued in *Feminist Theory: From Margin to Center* that issues of race and class must be taken on as part of feminism.

Beverley Bryan, Stella Dadzie and Suzanne Scafe discussed the experiences of Black women in Britain in *The Heart of the Race*. They argued that to understand Black women's lives today they must be seen within the history of British **imperialism** (making other countries into colonies and treating them unjustly) and involvement in the slave trade, which was done for economic gain.

Black feminism, which has a long history rooted in the movement to abolish slavery – the **Abolitionist Movement** – celebrates Black women's lives rather than portraying them as victims. It moves feminism beyond a **Eurocentric view** (seeing things only from the point of view of Europeans and their descendants) to bring in issues and voices of women in and from the developing world.

Liberal feminists

Liberal feminists believe in individual equal rights for women. All the other kinds of feminists mentioned above want to overturn the present social system in one way or another. Unlike them, liberal feminists want to work within the system, to reform it through equal rights laws, especially in areas like politics, employment and education. They want to end discrimination and build positive role models for women and girls.

Seeing women's discrimination as based solely on prejudice, liberal feminists believe this discrimination can be ended within our present system, without having to make major structural changes to it. They see change coming about through a gradual process and try to influence government to move this process along.

Betty Friedan, the founder of the National Organisation of Women in the United States and author of *The Feminine Mystique*, written in 1963, played a major role in sparking modern liberal feminism. It is especially popular in the US. But liberal feminism has a long history which goes back to Mary Wollstonecraft's *A Vindication of the Rights of Woman*, which she wrote, in 1792, in Britain.

EXERCISE 1.5
Looking at different feminist views

1 In what ways do you agree with and/or disagree with each of the feminist views mentioned above?
2 Which of them do you feel closest to? Why?

A glimpse of women's studies

I have only given you a brief look at the different feminist perspectives. Exploring further, you will find there are complex issues and various opinions within each group. You may want to look into the ideas which interest you the most.

Excerpts from the works of many of the authors mentioned in this chapter and elsewhere in the book can be found in *Feminisms – a Reader* edited by Maggie Humm and *Women's Studies – a Reader* edited by Stevi Jackson.

Although there are different positions within feminism individual women don't have to fit into one or another of them. As I mentioned earlier, some women don't even think the divisions are so clear cut nowadays. But understanding these perspectives will be useful in seeing various topics from different feminist points of view later in the book. Feminists from various standpoints often work together on projects and campaign on a wide variety of issues from abortion to child care and from rape to equal pay.

2

WOMEN'S HISTORY

Women's history is like a wondrous, rediscovered quilt. Its beauty lies in its diversity of texture, form and colour; offering us the depth and width of knowledge of our sisters throughout the world and throughout time. Our warm and comforting quilt helps us to learn about our past and brings us together through understanding. Together we can create our own patterns and sew in more of the missing pieces, ensuring that our daughters will not have to find the quilt all over again.

What is history?

Is history a record of the truth? Does it tell us what is most valuable about the past? If you and a friend you spent the day with last week each tried to honestly tell what happened, would your stories be the same? They certainly wouldn't be exactly the same. So which one is the real truth? Is there one real truth in retelling the past or just various **perceptions** (the way you see things) and **interpretations** (the meaning you put on things)? If there is no absolute truth, can history at least be a record of what is most valuable? But who decides what is most valuable? Why do the retelling of some events land in the history books, while others land in the dustbin?

Who makes history?

It is often said that in war, history is made by the victors. They are the ones with the power to keep their side of the story going. But people who have been conquered pass their stories down and try to keep them alive. Still you won't find their version in the history books of the victors. In that way history is made by those with the power to convince most people that their way of seeing things is correct. Or we can say that there is more than one history of any time, each based on different values and ways of seeing things.

There has always been a rich and exciting women's history. But we have generally been kept from knowing about our past because it would be a source of strength. Male-dominated society has kept this knowledge and its power from us, convincing us instead that it is male experience which we should value.

What is women's history?

Women's history is looking at the stories and achievements of all women. It is a rich, diverse subject profiting from the fact that women live in all countries and are a part of so many different groups. It's exciting to think about the range and possibilities of work in uncovering the knowledge of our past. Examining it with our own eyes we not only gain insight into the past, but we gain power and knowledge about the present. It can also help us to understand and build our future.

How do women go about finding their history?

If our history has been hidden, how do we go about finding it? As detectives the first thing we have to do is find sources. A **source** is where information comes from. **Primary sources** (first-hand information) can be women telling us about their experiences (I used to love sitting at the kitchen table with my mother, having her tell me about when she was a girl); letters written about what someone did or saw, diaries, autobiographies, oral history tapes or your own experiences. **Secondary sources** (second-hand information which has one or more people between the person who saw, heard or did it and you) are everything from books on a subject to paintings and from newspaper or magazine articles to television documentaries.

Male-dominated history has been created from a limited view of sources. By taking a creative approach to finding sources and using them women have begun to uncover our history, yet again. Not only does this approach teach us about ourselves, it also broadens the field of history. For example, in studying the white settlement of the American West the use of women's diaries and letters has added a new dimension to our understanding of the period.

How have we been kept from the knowledge of our history?

If we have a rich history, which male-dominated society has kept from us, how did they get away with it? It sounds like no easy trick to keep so much from us. Looking at the ways they've done it, with some examples, will help put our lost history into perspective.

Setting the values and context of history

Historically male-dominated society has valued what men do and put them centre stage. At the same time it has devalued women's actions, seeing them only in relation to men. This has meant that findings and events have been interpreted in a limited way which is often incorrect. For example, as Rosalind Miles points in *The Women's History of the World* generations of male commentators have blinded themselves to the facts and their indirect meaning (or **implications**) about early woman. Instead they built up an idea on how things happened or came to be: a **theory** of Man the Hunter. This was used to justify male aggression. In the violent, non-co-operative Man the

Hunter fantasy, men, who invent the first tools for hunting and single-handedly feed the women and children who are their possessions, develop physically and mentally as human beings while women helplessly sit by minding the children. Recently women have challenged this theory and played a major role in defeating it. There have also been men who opposed this theory.

The importance of early woman

Based on evidence of material which remains from earlier times which **archaeologists** have studied and on studying remote tribes in which people today live much as they did in the Stone Age, we can see that early women were busy gathering food, making pottery and weaving baskets, making clothes and containers out of animal skins, building shelters, making tools, using plants for medicines, as well as doing child care and cooking. The gathering of food by women was very important. They didn't depended on men hunting for their food. In fact, women's gathering accounted for the vast majority of the food intake, as hunting was often unsuccessful.

From the earliest times women's gathering kept the tribe alive and meant that women had to develop skills to tell the difference between and remember various kinds of plants. Even before hunting, women used tools to dig up roots, break open nuts and pound woody plants to make them easier to chew.

As Elizabeth Fisher points out in *Women's Creation – Sexual Evolution and the Shaping of Society*, it was early women's gathering which led them to invent needed household equipment. The first invention is thought to be a kind of container or sling to hold the various bits and pieces of food which women gathered. This could also hold a baby, leaving their hands free for gathering. The second invention was probably the digging stick.

Tools which used to be seen as weapons for hunting have, in recent years, been looked at again in the light of changing gender values in which early woman's role and her work has been viewed as having great importance. As the aggressive myth of Man the Hunter fades, we see instead more co-operation between early men and women in the process of changing, growing and surviving. Women played an essential role in this process in which they experimented with science for keeping fire, cooking and later firing pottery. Their work developed group activities, involved communication and led to a tribal culture. At times they were also involved in hunting, which was a group activity.

Looking at early peoples in this broader context, in which women's activities are valued, gives us a more realistic picture of our past.

Silencing our past

Although misinterpreting history is one way of keeping us from knowing about our achievements, we've mainly been kept from our past by the pure force of male history denying that it ever happened. By controlling knowledge, powerful men have decided what should be considered 'important' enough to pass on, based on male values. When such men set the rules and judge the game, women are not even counted. What women's movements have done over the ages is not agree to their rules. Image what a threat this has been to male-dominated power. No wonder they have kept us from the knowledge of these uprisings. They wouldn't want to give us any ideas of what could be possible if the rules were set fairly. Surely their power rests on stacking the cards against us. So recounting women's experience threatens the very rules of the game. By rediscovering our history, we gain power over our lives and help to change the boundaries of what is important.

EXERCISE 2.1 **Your view of history**

1 What does women's history mean to you?
2 How do you see yourself in relationship to history in general?
3 What do you think about the nature of history?

Voices in the silence

Our history has followed a pattern of being silenced, rediscovered and then silenced yet again. This makes it difficult to see where our ideas came from, creating the illusion that we keep starting from scratch, reinventing ourselves, many times over. And yet out there in the silence are all these wondrous voices of women, speaking in many languages, through the ages.

The hidden history of mother goddesses

As an example of our lost past, let us begin by looking at the hidden history of goddess-worship, which was practised by many different peoples through out the world. Rosalind Miles points out that one of the best-kept secrets of history is that for thousands of years, over much of the world, people worshipped some form of a Great Mother Goddess. Goddess-worship has been documented to have existed over a period of well over 25,000 years. From as early as 25,000 BC so-called 'Venus figures' were made of stone and ivory in Europe and of clay in Egypt. Although different names and forms were used, by 3000 BC mother goddesses appeared in shrines, statues and written records throughout the known world. In Africa and Australia; in Europe from Southern Russia, throughout the Mediterranean and in Asia as far as China; the Great Mother Goddess was in full control in human myths. This meant that women were seen to be powerful.

A belief in a Great Mother Goddess is thought to have begun as human beings moved beyond a struggle for mere survival. Their need for meaning focused on the wonders of birth and the ability of things to grow. Both of these marvels were linked to women. Not only did women give birth to new life, but they had progressed from gathering to planting, keeping their important role as the main producers of food. Women produced babies from their own bodies and crops from the body of the earth. As the power of nature was seen to be female the idea of a Great Mother grew.

In different versions, with different names and forms, the Great Goddess gave life. In India, Mata-Devi fed humans from the milk of her breasts. In both Polynesia and Assyria the Great Mother delivered a 'world egg'. And in Greece, Eleusis gave birth to corn each year.

The Goddess was more than a loving mother. As the controller of life, she controlled death. The Goddess had strength and all-mighty power. And as a woman she enjoyed and controlled her sexuality. In all the different cultural versions, the Great Goddess was never a wife. She had many lovers.

What a different vision women of that time had of what it meant to be female. For when God was female, society took its values and rhythms from women. Menstruation was not a curse, but a mysterious 'moon-gift from the Goddess' and the colour red was used in burial services. Women were seen as representing or coming from the Goddess and her power was passed down from mother to daughter. Queens passed on their power to their daughters and although a queen's husband was king, he had to yield to his daughter when his wife died. We see the power coming from the female line during ancient times in societies as diverse as those from the Celtic Britons to Japan (Wei dynasty) and from the Natchez Indians of the Gulf of Mexico to the Egyptians.

Ordinary women also had power over their lives. Women owned property and controlled their own money. They were not 'owned' in marriage but were respected as partners who were free to divorce. Like the Great Goddess, individual women controlled and enjoyed their sexuality. Not only did they train and compete in sports but women fought as front-line soldiers. And queens led their troops in battle.

When women were powerful during the period of goddess-worship they did not treat men the way they were later treated. The disproved theory, by some male historians, that societies ruled by women were overthrown by men and turned into patriarchies in which men only did to women what had been done to them, has been used to justify male domination over women. But **matriarchy** is better defined as a woman-centred form of social organisation, which was basically egalitarian, where it wasn't unusual for women to hold power or be involved in any part of society with men. Using this definition, we find there were large numbers of matriarchies or societies with matriarchal features (where women enjoyed freedoms).

Goddess-worship often lasted until it was suppressed by God the Father religions. Although societies and mythologies were different, generally there was a power-shift over time. They often moved from seeing the Goddess as all powerful to having a male God who became most powerful, with the Goddess still having some power. These changes tended to mirror the move to heavier agriculture (which was taken over by men) and the accumulation of wealth, although these were not the only factors.

As we rediscover our past power, we find that women were not always seen as inferior or 'unclean'. It was changing power relationships and values which forced that role upon us. Seeing that society's values can change so dramatically strengthens the belief in the possibility of the rules of the game being overturned to create equality. It also gives us an opportunity to question the values which we have internalised – to come to see ourselves, other women and the female image as powerful.

Using various sources to reconstruct the history of women in ancient India

As Uma Chakravarti and Kum Kum Roy point out in their contribution to the book *Retrieving Women's History*, even the way women's history has been silenced is different in different cultures and societies. Through an understanding of the culture of India, keeping in mind the difficulties of its long period of British colonisation, they look at the ways in which Indian women's past is being reconstructed.

Uma Chakravarti and Kum Kum Roy begin by looking at the way Ancient Indian women have been portrayed in general history books. If a ruler's wife played an influential role she is considered to be manipulative. Ruling queens are treated differently, depending on their relationship to men. Razia Sultan was the only woman to legally succeed to a throne and at that time was seen by many as a just and wise ruler, but she is not given respect today. On the other hand, Lakshmibai, who as regent queen took strong action in fighting against a foreign power to save her throne for her young son, is seen as the heroine of India. In general women are only seen within the family and those few women who are mentioned in the context of male history lead the reader to believe that women have played a minor role rather than that the history books have left them out.

Uma Chakravarti and Kum Kum Roy go through different historical sources looking for a clearer picture of women's history, which was left out of general history books. They point out that ancient books were mostly written by the special caste of Brahmanas who made the rules and were prejudiced against women. But recently Brahmanical texts have been used to look at different ways in which women were treated unfairly contrasting this view of ancient Indian women with the earlier idealised one.

Although much of Indian history is based on the books written by the Brahmanas, using other sources helps shed light on ancient Indian women. A Buddhist text called the *Therigatha* is thought to be the earliest book written by women. It is a useful source because the group of women who wrote it talk about the way they saw things. Buddhist sources have also been used to gain information about ancient women workers (outside their family) and about Buddhist nuns.

Uma Chakravarti has looked at the lives of women farm labourers on large land holdings and servants in the houses of the rich. Going back two thousand years, she's shown the contribution these women have made.

Another source has been the study of mother-goddess cults. This has been combined with the study of ancient myths to look at the change from a time when women had power to a male-dominated society.

Comparing ancient myths with more modern versions has proved to be an excellent source not only for seeing the changing role of women but in helping women to find stronger female models in the earlier versions of the stories. For example the original story of the heroine Sita, who is seen as a female model, has changed dramatically over time. Additions to the story have been used to shape Indian women's identity into a more passive role.

Uma Chakravarti and Kum Kum Roy want to change the focus of Indian history so that it includes household work, giving birth and raising children, collectively termed **social reproduction**. By looking at the history of sexuality with women's production (work outside their family responsibilities) and social reproduction, they hope to develop a more meaningful history of India.

Throughout the world women are looking at sources within their own cultures to develop a clearer picture of their history.

EXERCISE 2.2
Finding your history – looking for sources

1 What would you most like to know about your history? How could you find out about it?
2 What kind of primary sources could you use? Do you have contact with other women, perhaps older than yourself, who could help you? What about your own experiences?
3 What secondary sources can you use? What libraries or other resources do you have access to?

Glimpses of women's resistance, power and achievement

With so much of women's history to choose from, I have decided to pick out different models of women's resistance, power and/or achievements, which not only give a flavour of the past, but also help us understand the present and imagine the future. These models were often created in pockets of opportunities for women which were later closed down or there were women's movements which then ended. Sometimes women made massive gains, other times they were crushed. Because our history has gone in cycles, with an enormous effort made by the powers of male-dominated society to bury the knowledge of our positive accomplishments in the down side of the cycle, we must be careful about the way we judge these models.

Even if a social movement like a co-operative action or a strike is crushed, does that mean it was a failure? What about the lessons it teaches us for the future? Any resistance is a success in the sense that it shows us what is possible. All the models that I describe, whether they reached their goal or even had a well-defined one, were successful in showing us what women can do – in helping us imagine greater expectations for ourselves, thus changing expectations of women; and in showing how we can organise and create things in new ways, setting our own rules of the game. We should celebrate every woman who struggled to live with dignity against oppression, especially respecting those women who were most deeply oppressed and still managed to hold their head up high.

Not all women were treated the same

One of the most striking things that we see as our past comes to light is that all women were not treated the same. Sheila Rowbotham points out in books such as *Hidden from History* that although all women were held back, women from different economic classes were treated differently. She highlights the important role that economics has played, specifically looking at how under capitalism, men's power has been used to control women's labour in the family as well as the public workplace. She focuses on the oppression of working-class women.

In *Women, Race and Class*, Angela Davis examines the experiences of

Black women in slavery to rediscover how Black women have always resisted white oppression. Not only does she challenge white and Black male histories of slavery, but she also challenges white feminist ideas. Angela Davis shows how Black women have gained strength from their role as a mother in the family and as part of a community, which has been a helpful support in the harsh public workplace.

In *Not a Passing Phase* the Lesbian History Group points out that lesbian history is not only rediscovering the lives of women who have experienced their love for other women (whatever form that took and whatever they called themselves). It is an approach to history which looks at how anti-lesbianism has been used. This has meant that lesbian experience has either been suppressed or presented not for what it is but as a form of perversion. The Lesbian History Group looks at the past using their own vision and definitions to examine women's lives and to see how they were treated by society.

Recent work on the diverse history of women has helped us to see the importance of factors other than gender when looking at the oppression of women.

European medieval women build their freedom in towns

In *Women in the Medieval Town*, Erika Uitz points out that in Europe, between the twelfth and sixteenth centuries, women who could escape to a town and stay there for a year and a day were granted their freedom from their feudal lord. The growth of towns created a need for workers and women did everything from trading and banking to mining and sword making. Because women's skills were valued they began to gain some independence and some financial power in and out of marriage, along with sexual and financial protection against the nobility. Although women were often poor, paid less than men for the same work (including construction work) and were expected to act in a 'feminine' way, they developed a variety of skills and showed their talents and creativity, illuminating manuscripts, spinning gold thread, painting dolls, binding books and making candles, barrels and crates. In some French towns women started their own organisations of skilled workers, or guilds. Other guilds were opened up to women, who became mistresses of their own apprentices.

Christine de Pisan, a Venetian woman born in 1364, wrote the *Book of the City of Ladies*, in which she spoke out against women being seen as inferior and the *Book of Three Virtues*, where she argued for the education of all women.

During this period of change, where women workers were needed in towns, we find a pattern which was often repeated in history. Women show their capabilities only to have their history buried, so that they can later be told that they are incapable of the very things which they had been doing for centuries.

Women in revolutions

Revolution is born out of a thrust for justice. In such a time of change, when so many of the old rules have broken down, it is only natural that women should demand justice. They did this in America and France in the eighteenth century, just as in the twentieth century women have played leading roles in liberation struggles in developing nations.

Women in the American Revolution

Women were active in early revolutionary movements in America. In Bacon's rebellion of 1676, a hundred years before the successful American revolution, it was a women lieutenant who first gathered Bacon's followers and acted as his emissary. Another woman, Mistress Sarah Drummond, reacted to the British governor's death threats by breaking a stick under his nose and telling him, 'I fear the power of England no more than a broken straw!' Clearly, being a pioneer in the New World broke down some of the old rules.

In the consumer boycott of British tea and other goods in 1769, women were the crucial participants who even made the cloth that the colonists then needed. Although many women supported the revolutionary war the call for no taxation without representation had special meaning for them. This is clear from Abigail Adams' letter of 31 March 1776 to her husband, John Adams (who later became the second President), in which she tells him to 'Remember the Ladies' when making new laws. She says 'If particular care and attention is not paid to the Ladies we are determined to foment a rebellion, and will not hold ourselves bound by any Laws in which we have no voice, or Representation.'

Women in the French Revolution

Women played a strong role in the French Revolution. It was a woman, Théroigne de Méricourt, dressed as an Amazon, who led the storming of the Bastille. Later that year she led over 6000 women through Paris, demanding bread. On that Day of the Market Women they marched to Versailles. Women stormed the national assembly and then overran the palace, taking Marie Antoinette and her family back to Paris as prisoners of the people. It was the women who triggered the French Revolution with their actions. In doing so they also broke many of their gender bonds. Women's political clubs were formed and female 'citizens' participated in the revolutionary debates.

Early in the revolution when the Declaration of the Rights of Man was produced, Olympe de Gouges wrote the *Declaration of the Rights of Women* calling for women to have the same rights as men and denouncing men's supposed superiority as an empty pretence. She demanded that women be given full political rights, including being able to run for parliament and hold any public office. She argued that women's lack of education was keeping them in low-paid jobs, which forced them to marry or become prostitutes, and kept them from being considered equal under the law. Olympe de Gouges believed that the institution of marriage had failed and should be replaced by a fairer arrangement. She also opposed revolutionary men who oppressed women saying, 'Man, the slave, has multiplied his strength...Once free, he became unjust to his companion...What advantages have you [women] got from the Revolution? A more open contempt!'

When the Jacobins came to power Olympe de Gouges was guillotined with many others for opposing their leader, Robespierre. He denied women the vote when it was given to all men, forced the women's political clubs to disband and terrorised women back into the home. Although once again we see the cycle of women's history return to the down side, the achievements of French Revolutionary Women and their insights about their gender were not lost forever. In fact, as often happened their deeds and declarations served to inspire women elsewhere.

Mary Wollstonecraft and the rights of women

The women's movement is often seen to start with Mary Wollstonecraft, as if she alone and for the first time, was able to see and discuss our oppression. I don't think Mary Wollstonecraft would have agreed with that idea, nor do I think it devalues her important contributions to see her in context. So why has she been pictured this way in the history books? Dale Spender argues in *Women of Ideas* that if Mary Wollstonecraft, Catherine Macaulay and Mary Hays (who were all writing about women's rights towards the end of the eighteenth century) were studied together, they could well be seen as the start of a women's movement; but the idea of a 200-year-old movement which is still basically fighting the same battles would be too threatening for patriarchal society. Spender believes that the interests of patriarchy are better served if the occasional female is portrayed as making unreasonable demands which are not seen to represent most women.

When Mary Wollstonecraft wrote her important book *A Vindication of the Rights of Woman* in 1792, Olympe de Gouges was still alive and active in France, having already written the *Declaration of the Rights of Women*. Change was in the air, women in England had begun to be published and speak out for their gender and Mary Wollstonecraft became a spokesperson for British women's thrust for justice.

In *A Vindication of the Rights of Woman*, Mary Wollstonecraft questioned the very basis of male authority over women. She showed how men misused the ideas of reason and truth to justify their power and sense of superiority over women, making them dependent on men. Mary Wollstonecraft took on respected male thinkers, like Rousseau, showing how their own words about women's inferiority were illogical. She called on women to have strong minds and bodies; to reject their passive, pleasing role, as she had done, and to have power over their lives, looking at the world from their own point of view.

Her strong defiant words brought a storm of criticism, though there were also those who defended her. Because she was a woman who led an unconventional life, getting involved with the French Revolution, having affairs and a child out of marriage, she was attacked not only for her views but for her personal actions. Basically she was such a threat that they had to attack her. But her courageous outspoken ideas have lived on through the centuries. She died giving birth to a daughter, who later became Mary Wollstonecraft Godwin Shelley and wrote the famous work of science-fiction, *Frankenstein*.

Black women in slavery – resistance to dehumanisation

Dehumanisation is trying to take away people's human qualities.

As Beverley Bryan, Stella Dadzie and Suzanne Scafe point out in *The Heart of the Race*, Black women in slavery used their African heritage and their communal experience to resist the process of dehumanisation which not only came at them because of racism and the economic basis of slavery, but also because they were women. As women they worked a 'double day' producing wealth for their owners and being involved with social reproduction. Their resistance took many forms from outright rebellion to 'birth strikes'. As workers and mothers they played a leading role in building and maintaining a culture which kept alive the ability to celebrate life and thus survive. What an amazing accomplishment in the face of the brutality which was heaped upon Black women by those who called themselves civilised.

In the Caribbean most Black women slaves were agricultural field workers, others did domestic work. Women were expected to work as hard and as many hours as men, with no recognition for their additional responsibilities. Especially while the slave trade was legal, generally four or five hours was all the time they were given not only to sleep but for their other tasks, even when women were pregnant or had just given birth. Slaves were not only overworked but malnourished and medically neglected and yet women, with their extra burdens, generally lived longer than men. Even with this stamina, women's lives in slavery were short as it was seen to be more 'profitable' to work slaves to death and then to replace them. Against this life-threatening dehumanisation, based on seeing Black women as expendable economic chattel, resistance was dangerous and difficult.

The resistance of Black women in slavery was born out of their traditions in Africa. From Nzinga, the warrior queen who fought the Portuguese in the early seventeenth century, to the Queen Mothers of the Ashanti wars against the British, African women played a powerful role in resistance. Generally their role in tribal societies was one in which they played an important part in trading and agriculture, while creating crafts and medicines and being responsible for their children. Their pride in their own value within their African society and their sense of community responsibility not only helped them survive and resist within slavery, it also resulted in them leaving a strong oral history for those who came after them.

Black women's resistance in slavery took many forms, including individual acts. Any resistance took an enormous amount of courage as it risked being whipped, or killed. And women were punished as often and as brutally as men. But when flogging was finally outlawed by the British in the 1820s the Governor of Trinidad, Sir Ralph Woodford, wrote to the Colonial Secretary in London complaining that countless incidents 'of insolence and insubordination occur frequently among the female slaves' and that he no longer had the power 'to repress the violence of turbulent women'. Domestic slaves also played a role in resistance, doing everything from trying to poison the owner's food to secretly learning to read and write, which was forbidden, then passing on information from newspapers and books to other slaves.

Slave owners tried to control women's reproductive role, based on their own economic needs, which women resisted. After the slave trade was abolished in British West Indian colonies in 1807 and no new slaves could be brought to the Caribbean from Africa, slave owners looked to women to reproduce their labour force. But many women resisted being used as breeders. They used breastfeeding as a form of natural contraception and as passive resistance to long hours of work. Other reasons for women's low birth-rate included mistreatment such as injuries from excessive beatings, illness, overwork and malnutrition. The physical mistreatment of Black women slaves has been likened to the experience of women in Nazi concentration camps, who also suffered a loss of fertility.

Women slaves played an important role in uprisings and organised rebellions. In the inaccessible region of Jamaica known as the Maroons, there were many women who escaped slavery and went there to become guerrillas. Nanny of Maroon Town played a leadership role in the Maroon Wars of 1733. Not only did she direct guerrilla actions she also played a spiritual role. By the end of the eighteenth century more women were living in the Maroons than men. Cubah 'Queen of Kingston' was another resistance leader.

Women played a major role in keeping the Creole language alive and passing it down to their children. Creole, a forbidden language created by Black slaves, was used to build community and create a means of communication amongst slaves from diverse parts of Africa. Power was gained in having a language, not understood by the owners, which was used for resistance.

Abolitionist basis of US Women's Rights Movement

The Women's Rights Movement in the US was born out of the

movement to abolish slavery, just as later the Civil Rights Movement in the 1960 served as the inspiration for the Second Wave of Feminism in US. In 1833 Sarah Mapp Douglass, a Black schoolteacher, founded the Female Anti-Slavery Society with other Black and white Quaker women including Lucretia Mott.

Lucretia Mott and Elizabeth Cady Stanton were both barred from attending the International Anti-Slavery Convention in England in 1840 because they were female delegates. As *Feminism for Beginners* documents, their exclusion inspired them to campaign for the rights of women. This led them to organise the first Women's Rights Convention in Seneca Falls, New York in 1848. When some men tried to break up the convention by heckling, a Black woman named Sojourner Truth helped to save the convention with the following speech:

> That man over there says women need to be helped into carriages, and lifted over ditches, and to have the best place everywhere. Nobody ever helps me into carriages, and lifted me over ditches, or over mud-puddles, or gives me any best place! And ain't I a woman? Look at me! Look at my arm! I have ploughed, and planted, and gathered into barns, and no man could head me! And ain't I a woman? I could work as much and eat as much as a man – when I could get it – and bear the lash as well! And ain't I a woman? I have borne thirteen children, and seen most all sold off to slavery, and when I cried with my mother's grief, none but Jesus heard me! And ain't I a woman?

When a clergyman used the familiar argument that men were superior because Jesus Christ was a man, Sojourner Truth (who was a travelling preacher) countered by asking where Jesus Christ came from in the first place. 'God and a woman – *man* had nothing to do with it.'

After a hotly contested argument at the convention, Elizabeth Cady Stanton's resolution to campaign for the vote was passed. Following the convention, Elizabeth Cady Stanton teamed up with Susan B. Anthony, who was single and able to be a travelling organiser while Elizabeth Cady Stanton wrote speeches at home as she cared for her eight children. The courage and persistence of many women during that period, facing heckling and sometimes violent mobs as well as massive disapproval, enabled them to successfully pressure many state legislatures to grant women some financial rights, such as working women having their wages paid to them rather than to their husband. These women also served as an inspiration to women of future generations as they struggled not only for the vote but for financial and legal independence, as well as full educational rights.

By working to end slavery, free Black and white women came to a greater understanding of their oppression as women, although their relationship to racism meant that they had different perspectives on this. They used the skills they had developed as abolitionists, and the belief that change was possible, to build a movement for women's freedom. Over a hundred years later, as a young woman living in the US, I saw how the ripples of change created by the Civil Rights Movement empowered a generation of women to believe that we too had the power to dream of equality and act to change our lives.

The British Women's Movement

In Britain in the early nineteenth century, women lacked many basic rights. It was just about impossible for married women to get a divorce, no matter what their husbands did to them. Even if a man left his wife, she could neither get custody of her children or own property. Women had very few chances for education or independence. Middle-class wives were trapped in their houses with their husbands having enormous power over them. Working-class women were generally very low-paid, often badly treated domestic servants or industrial workers.

Working-class women began to organise for their rights. They started women's unions such as the Edinburgh Upholsterers Sewers Society in 1872 and the National Union of Working Women in Bristol in 1874. In that same year Emma Paterson started the Women's Protection and Provident League, which helped women unionise and win strikes such as the strike of woollen weavers in Dewsbury, Yorkshire. Other women took up the idea and in 1875 all-women unions were formed in London. The national Women's Co-operative Guild also played an important role.

Women carried out a good number of industrial actions between 1888 and 1892. The matchgirls' strike was well publicised. Other militant actions were carried out by women blanket weavers, cotton workers, cigarmakers and jute workers. In London women in a tin box factory even threw flour and red-ochre at men who wouldn't come out on strike with them.

Women were a necessary part of the textile industry. In places like Lancashire, where they were cotton workers, they even organised some short-lived women's trade societies as early as the 1830s. Although they were kept from the higher paying technical jobs, which were reserved for men, by the end of the nineteenth century women cotton workers were better paid and better organised than other working women. Often the justification for women's low wages was the idea of a 'family wage', which would only be paid to a male breadwinner. In Lancashire this idea was not as strong and women went on to organise for better conditions including the right to vote.

Middle-class women fought for their legal and financial rights. In 1839 the fight for child custody, led by Caroline Norton, brought in The Infant Custody Act. But this only gave women their children if they were under 7 years old. In 1882 The Married Women's Property Act meant that wives could finally own property and control their own money. But since it was so hard for women to earn much money this, too, had a limited gain. In order to make real changes women knew they needed a voice in parliament, so they began to focus on gaining the vote.

The suffrage movement in Britain and the issue of class
In Britain the campaign for female **suffrage** (that is the right to vote) was complicated by the fact that some working-class men also did not have the right to vote. So British women had to decide whether to fight for adult suffrage, the right to vote for both men and women, or for limited women's suffrage, which would mean that only certain women (such as those who owned property) could vote.

In 1900 Millicent Fawcett brought together many of the women's suffrage societies spread throughout Britain in the National Union of Women's Suffrage Societies to work for women's suffrage. This large, mostly middle-class, movement used legal, moderate tactics. They patiently created a network of democratic women's suffrage societies, working within the established system and holding huge demonstrations.

In 1903 Emmeline Pankhurst and her daughters, Christabel and Sylvia formed the Women's Social and Political Union with some women from the Independent Labour Party. But when parliamentary means failed they turned militant, using direct action to try to gain women's suffrage. Women were often jailed. When they went on hunger strikes they were tortured by force feeding. They courageously kept up their fight. A variety of tactics was used including holding demonstrations and mass torch-light processions with waged and unwaged women, smashing the windows of government buildings, chaining themselves to the Downing Street railings, breaking into the Prime Minister's car to lecture him on 'Votes for Women' and organising women in communities such as London's East End to demand equal pay and decent housing, as well as the vote.

Working-class women who fought for the vote as part of a larger campaign for better wages and working conditions for women plus improved conditions for working-class mothers and children have been called Radical Suffragists. This term was coined by Jill Liddington and Jill Norris in their book about Lancashire women entitled *One Hand Tied Behind Us*. Radical Suffragists demanded 'womanhood suffrage', which would mean votes for all adult women. The only way the government would ever do this was if they granted adult suffrage both to men and women, but the Radical Suffragists focused on the women's demand. As trade unionists their tactics included factory gate meetings; getting womanhood suffrage motions passed at local union branches, trades councils and Women's Co-operative Guild branches; and working through the Labour Party. As respected union organisers, women like Selina Cooper, Helen Silcock and Sarah Reddish were able to push for womanhood suffrage and women's political power at a national level.

Working-class women also continued their struggle for their rights in the workplace. More women's organisations were established as many women were unrecognised by existing trade unions. Mary Macarthur, the president of the Scottish section of the Shop Assistants' Union, helped to start the National Federation of Women Workers in 1906. By 1916 it had 60,000 women members.

During the First World War more and more men were dying as soldiers in the front-lines, so women were needed to do all kinds of war work. Although they had previously been told they were incapable of these traditionally male jobs, women did everything from driving buses to working in engineering and munitions factories. Though they were usually paid less to do the same work, their wages did go up and they gained some welfare benefits. They joined unions and men were forced to take them seriously. Much of the women's movement urged women to take up 'men's jobs' to show that they were equal to the work and the vote. Other women were against the war, including the Radical Suffragists, Sylvia Pankhurst and those women who split off from the National Union of Women's Suffrage Societies led by Helena Swanwick, who formed the Women's International League for Peace and Freedom.

When the war ended in 1918 certain categories of women over 30 years old won the right to vote. Although this included many women over 30 it meant that there were still women who had run essential services during the war who were not considered capable of voting. In 1928 all women from the age of 21 gained the vote. The fight for the vote stimulated other women's movements and helped women win some legal rights such as the right to divorce a husband on the grounds of adultery and the right to become an MP, judge or lawyer.

The contributions of Irish women

Because of England's history of colonising Ireland and because of the Great Famine of 1845–9, large numbers of women were forced to leave Ireland in order to survive, earn a living and often to send money home to their families. Although the immediate reason for the famine was a blight that destroyed the potato crop, which the peasant people were forced to depend on, three-quarters of Irish cultivable land was being used to grow cereals, almost all of which was shipped to England along with grazing animals while about two million people starved or died of related diseases. One and a half million people emigrated from Ireland during the Famine, many of whom were women with their families. After the Famine the structure of rural life changed and large numbers of single women began bravely emigrating by themselves. Many of them came to work in Britain taking on exhausting, low-paid jobs, living in terrible conditions and often sending money home to help their families.

Ann Rossiter points out that although more research is needed about the lives of these women, it is important to credit the contributions of Irish working women to Britain. As field labourers, they often moved from place to place, taking on other jobs including mining and smelting work in the iron furnaces of South Wales. Irish women made an important contribution to the manufacturing of textiles. Many women worked in the cotton industry in Manchester and Wigan. In Scotland large numbers of skilled Irish women were textile workers in Greenock, and in Dundee they were jute and linen workers. In

London, as well as being street sellers (especially of fruit) they were skilled needle workers in the clothing trade and semiskilled manufacturing workers. Irish women often went into domestic service throughout Britain, working in highly exploited positions as general servants, casual cleaners and laundry workers.

Mary Feeney argues that the limited kinds of work which Irish women in Britain were allowed to do contrasts greatly with the abilities they demonstrated when given the opportunity. She cites the example of the Ladies Land League. In January 1881, in Ireland, the Ladies Land League was formed as a female branch of the Land League, which campaigned for the rights of tenant farmers. As more and more of the men in the Land League were arrested the women took over. Anna Parnell was the leader of the Ladies Land League. For eighteen months the women directed a mass movement of tenant farmers. Their work included campaigning, organising a rent strike and the building of wooden huts to shelter evicted tenant-farmer families, compiling records and organising financial matters including supporting tenant-farmer families on rent strike. By the beginning of 1882 there were over 500 branches of the Ladies Land League all over Ireland and some in Scotland and England.

Although women in the Ladies Land League in Ireland demonstrated their abilities, in Britain Irish women in domestic service were often kept from direct contact with their employers, an explanation given for this is that they were seen as inferior. Nineteenth-century theories about 'race', which have since been completely discredited, set out the idea that inherited 'race' differences not only involved how people looked but also their character. This was used as an excuse for colonising other countries. A hierarchy was set up which put Anglo-Saxons at the top, Black people at the bottom and Celts and Jews somewhere in between.

Jewish women garment workers lead the Uprising of 20,000

At the end of the nineteenth century and the beginning of the twentieth century large numbers of Jewish immigrants came to the United States from what is now Russia and Poland to escape **pogroms** (organised anti-Semitic massacres) and for economic reasons. In order to survive in the US many Jewish women, especially those who were young and unmarried, went to work in the garment industry in New York, often sewing in sweatshops or working in textile factories. By the end of the nineteenth century the majority of garment workers were Jewish women. The work they did was exhausting, with terrible conditions and employer abuses. Women also had the longest hours and the lowest pay. Salary deductions were taken for petty things like electricity, sewing machine needles and minor rule infractions at the employer's whim.

As Silja Joanna Aller Talvi points out, Jewish women garment workers began to organise against these awful conditions. They were part of a working-class movement which also involved radical political groups – socialists and anarchists. Meeting in smoke-filled cafes, Jewish women not only discussed their struggles in the workplace but also radical politics, the friction between Jewish tradition and female emancipation and the need to distribute birth control information in Yiddish. Out of this atmosphere came 'new' radical Jewish women who were sometimes referred to as 'the battlers'.

Between 1880 and 1908, although Jewish women organised strikes and other actions in the workplace, they were generally unrecognised by the male trade union movement. In 1909, as the economy improved, the militancy of Jewish women led to a massive strike called the Uprising of 20,000. It mainly involved Jewish women with others such as Italian women. The Uprising in New York began with two smaller strikes which were not having much success as the women were being beaten up by company thugs and arrested on the picket lines.

An open meeting was called in November 1909 to discuss a general strike of the Ladies' Waist Makers' Union Local 25 of the International Ladies' Garment Workers' Union. With thousands of people present and many trade union leaders urging caution, Clara Lemlich (a small young woman with passion in her large dark eyes), who was already on strike and recovering from a beating on the picket line, got up and declared in Yiddish, 'I have listened to all the speakers, and I have no further patience for talk. I am one who feels and suffers for the things pictured. I move that we go on a general strike!' She so inspired the crowd that they stood up clapping and shouting.

A general strike was proclaimed, closing down about five hundred shops with 20,000 women coming out on strike. The Women's Trade

Union League supported the strike with its leader, Rose Schneiderman, and thousands of other women braving the cold, the beatings by company thugs and brutal police arrests. As the police brutality escalated 30,000 women signed a petition demanding decent treatment by the police and wealthy suffragists joined the picket line and contributed to the strike fund. The actions of these suffragists helped to build publicity for the strike and develop links between various elements of the suffrage movement.

After more than nine weeks the strike ended with some gains including a lowering of the 60-hour work-week to 52 hours per week, time and a half for overtime and an end to charges for electricity, etc. But the main aims of the strike, including improvement in health and safety standards, were not achieved. And yet the spirit, determination and solidarity of those 20,000 women led to a stronger women's movement and more recognition within the trade union movement.

In 1911, 146 Jewish and Italian women died in a fire at the Triangle Shirtwaist Company because the health and safety demands of the strike had not been achieved. The funeral procession included 120,000 women and men with over 400,000 onlookers. Out of the shock and horror of the fire came the building of a stronger Jewish working-class movement and, within the following decade, improvements in health and safety laws.

A personal note

My grandmother, Ester Perlstein Magezis, was an organiser of the Women's Trade Union League and a leader of the Ladies' Waist Makers' Union. She worked as a sewing machine operator in one of those sweatshops I've described and was very active in the Uprising of 20,000. She was also a suffragist. But my Grandma Ester died before she could tell me about any of these women's movements which she cared about so deeply.

It is only now, writing this section, that I've been able to piece things together and get some flavour of my grandmother's life, bringing me closer to her. I can imagine her in those smoke-filled cafes arguing her point or speaking at meetings. But it's also been frustrating to research events which Grandma could have told me about. Perhaps if she hadn't been forced to work under such terrible conditions she'd have been alive long enough to tell me about her life and her work as an organiser.

What I remember about my grandmother is looking back at the window of her room as my father and I came out of the sheltered housing where she lived right before she died. My father told me to remember her. But all I remember is her hand on the lace curtain. For years I've wished I could remember more of her. But then, as I tried to find out about her work as an organiser, I suddenly viewed things differently. I had the feeling that perhaps that last time, as she looked out her window at my father and I walking down the stairs away from her she thought, 'That little *maidel*, maybe that one will make a difference for women'. I'll try Grandma. I'll try.

EXERCISE 2.3
How have you been affected by women's history?

1 What perspective have you gained about your own life by reading about women's history?
2 Has it changed the way you view your own history?

The history of International Women's Day

On 8 March 1907 women garment workers and war widows marched in New York for better working conditions and equal rights for women. As they reached a wealthy area of town the police broke up the demonstration, arresting many women. The following year, on the same date, there was a demonstration on the Lower East Side of New York by women working in the needle trades to commemorate the earlier revolt. They called for women's suffrage and an end to sweatshops and child labour. They were also met by police.

In 1910, Clara Zetkin proposed to the Second International Conference of Socialist Women in Copenhagen that 8 March be commemorated each year as International Women's Day in honour of the earlier struggles of working women in New York. Clara Zetkin led a large German Social Democratic Party Women's Movement which not only campaigned for the vote but also for equal access to work and co-education. Although police often broke up the demonstrations which the German socialist women held on International Women's Day the holiday spread worldwide. The Russian Revolution began on International Women's Day in 1917 with massive demonstrations and food protests by women and children. In the West the holiday mostly died out by the end of the 1930s, but with the rebirth of feminism, new life was breathed into the commemoration in the early 1970s. In 1978 it was officially recognised by the United Nations.

A sampling of the worldwide struggle for women's suffrage

The dawn of the twentieth century found women in many parts of the world fighting for their rights, often using suffrage as a focus for their demands. Women in New Zealand were the first to win the right to vote nationally in 1894. And from the Philippines, where Concepción Felix and Pura Villanueva Kalaw led a movement, to Sri Lanka, where Agnes de Silva led a campaign, women could be heard demanding the right to vote.

In Australia, white women in the state of South Australia gained the vote in 1894. Other states followed and by 1908 white women all over Australia were able to vote. The Australian Women's Political Association was formed in 1909 to educate women in using the vote and to fight for equal pay, equal rights in marriage and international suffrage and peace. Aboriginal Australian women and men did not gain the right to vote until 1967. Aboriginal women used the *jilimi* (a camp for widows, women who left their husbands and single women) as a place of solidarity and freedom, which was taboo to men.

In Japan, after Kishida Toshiko led the fight for women's rights and the vote at the end of the nineteenth century, the Seitoscha feminist group produced a magazine from 1911–16 looking at marriage and women's lives and calling for suffrage and other rights. In the 1920s Ichikawa Fusae organised a suffrage movement.

Although the Women's Indian Association was unsuccessful in pressuring the British for women's suffrage, in 1918 the Indian National Congress came out in support of women's right to vote. A number of women played important roles within the Indian National Congress and Pandita Ramabai formed women's organisations throughout the country. When India gained independence in 1947, all adults were given the vote.

Chinese women – unbound feet

In the early twentieth century women in China worked to improve their lives as part of playing an important role in creating overall political change. As Sheila Rowbotham points out in *Women in Movement*, beginning in the 1890s female factory workers held militant strikes against their terrible conditions. In 1906 Jiu Jin created the *Chinese Women's Journal*, calling for women's enslavement to be completely overturned, while also making explosives for the anti-Manchu dynasty revolution, which was successful in 1911.

With the success of the 1911 revolution and the creation of a constitution, the women's Chinese Suffragette Society not only demanded the vote and political rights but also the ending of the practice of binding women's feet, education and rights in the family. But in 1913 a warlord took power and protest was repressed until 1916. (The restriction of growth and therefore size of women's feet by binding them had traditionally been done in the name of beauty. Obviously it also restricted their lives.)

In 1919 women were active in the May Fourth student movement against Japanese imperialism and sparked debates around many women's issues. Socialist and Marxist ideas about the need for women's rights were linked with workers' rights. In 1921, when the Communist Party was formed, their women's magazine *Women's Voice* focused on rights for working women. Xiang Jingyu, leader of the Communist Party Women's Department, stressed both the need for many male workers to change their attitudes and for women workers to fight for their own freedom within the revolutionary process of change. Although both the Communists and Nationalists movements did not see how women getting the vote, with the regime which was in power, would solve women's massive social and economic problems, they each had active women's movements demanding changes in the family as well as economic and social equality.

In 1924 women students and workers held a small demonstration in Canton on International Women's Day calling for equal education, equal pay, an end to the sale of slave girls and an end to imperialism. In 1926 the Women's Unions, consisting of young women who cut their hair, wore trousers and went with Chiang Kai-Shek's army (who was fighting the warlords), were helping women stand up against their husbands and freeing slave girls and prostitutes. In 1927 the International Women's Day demonstration in Canton was 25,000 strong. But then the civil war started and in the anti-left-wing reaction over a thousand members of the Women's Union were killed.

During the Long March and for years afterwards, women Communists helped organise peasant women. As peasant women began meeting together and talking about their problems and experiences, they came to see their common grievances. They called this 'speaking bitterness' and 'exchanging experiences'. (Women in the US, in the late 1960s, were influenced by this form of organising when they began creating consciousness raising groups.) Peasant women moved from talking about their oppression to taking action as a group in their villages. They did everything from stopping husbands beating their wives to ending forced marriages. Each small success gave them more confidence in their own power.

The Nissàist Movement – Arabic feminism – the Egyptian experience

As Huda Shaarawi points out in *Harem Days – The Memoirs of an Egyptian Feminist*, by the beginning of the twentieth century, women in Egypt began to question their lives, in which they were secluded from the public world and fully veiled. Upper-class women in harems and middle-class women, as well, began to conclude that it was not the Muslim religion that required them to be veiled and kept apart from men but social custom. Women began to meet in private houses and then together in public halls. They argued that Islam should not be interpreted as being against women's rights, instead it was the customs of their society which were holding them back. (Today Muslim women, such as Fatima Mernissi in her article 'Women in Muslim history' published in *Retrieving Women's History*, make the same point. Not only do they show how the mass of religious historic evidence backs up their case for women's rights, but also the political nature of women's oppression.) In 1911 Malak Hifni Nasif became the first woman to make a public demand for women's rights at the Egyptian Congress in Heliopolis.

Women were involved in the growing nationalist movement against British occupation. This experience helped them create a public feminist movement. Huda Shaarawi, an upper-class woman who was married at 13 years old, against her wishes, became the president of the Wafdist Women's Central Committee and took an active role in the 1919 revolution against the British. In 1923, a year after Egyptian independence, she founded the Egyptian Feminist Union and led a delegation to a meeting of the International Alliance of Women in Rome. On her return she was met by a group of women at the Cairo railway station where in open defiance she publicly unveiled herself. Other women followed, creating an end to the harem system.

By the end of the 1920s the Egyptian Feminist Union had 250 members consisting both of middle- and upper-class women. They had two monthly journals and funded health care and craft workshop projects for poor women and a child care centre for working mothers. The Feminist Union successfully fought for a legal minimum marriage age and better educational opportunities for women, culminating in women entering Cairo university. They also demanded changes in the family, within Islamic law.

In the 1930s the Egyptian Feminist Union organised around the issues of working women in textile factories and shops, education and health. In the second half of the 1930s the feminist movement campaigned strongly for women's suffrage in Egypt. Attending an international meeting in France, Egyptian feminists campaigned for their French sisters who were also still fighting for the vote.

EXERCISE 2.4 **Examining women's history**

1 What do you find surprising about women's history?
2 What specific parts of it do you find empowering?
3 How is it disturbing?

An overview

The glimpses of women's history which I have highlighted show the enormous capability, strength and determination of women throughout the ages. I have focused very specifically on what women have done, although in a number of cases their actions were part of political movements involving both women and men. Women helped to create and build these political movements, but too often their contributions were either minimised or ignored in the history books.

I've only been able to give you a taste of women's history. But I hope this has whet your appetite for more. There is an enormous amount of recent women's history to be explored and chronicled for future generations, as well as women's history which is buried, waiting to be rediscovered.

EXERCISE 2.5 **Recording women's history**

1 Write about some part of women's history which interests you. Use your own experiences, books, oral histories or other sources.

2 Meet with other women who want to explore women's history and share your information and methods of finding it.

3 Try using the information you find as the basis of creative expression in a form such as art work, drama, creative writing or story telling.

3

WOMEN AND WORDS: LANGUAGE AND LITERARY CRITICISM

We want to use language to give voice to our lives in our own way. Beyond the limits of their rules we howl and rejoice to tell our own stories in our own words.

Language

Are words neutral?

Does it matter if you're called a 'woman', 'lady' or 'girl'?

EXERCISE 3.1

Read the sentences below. What is the difference in the image you get of the adult female described? In which example would she have the best chance of getting an interview?

1 I know a lady who's looking for work. Would you like to interview her for your job vacancy?
2 I know a girl who's looking for work. Would you like to interview her for your job vacancy?
3 I know a woman who's looking for work. Would you like to interview her for your job vacancy?

As Robin Lakoff points out in *Language and a Woman's Place*, using the word 'lady' makes the female subject seem less serious as far as being able to accomplish something important. In the first sentence above there could even be a suggestion of the lady looking for unpaid work to 'occupy her time'. The word 'lady' is often used to stand for someone who doesn't do heavy work. In this way it can help to divide 'genteel' and 'common' females which involves issues of class.

Now with the word 'girl' it can depend on whether it's a male or female using the term. Females can have non-sexual girlfriends, but men aren't said to have non-sexual boyfriends. If they go out with 'the boys' it's seen to mean they're being young and irresponsible. So what does that say about calling a working adult female a Girl Friday?

In the early 1970s grown women workers, such as secretaries, began objecting to being called a 'girl' by their male bosses, who were generally their age or younger. Just as using the word 'boy' when talking about a grown Black man in India or the southern United States was seen as a sign of disrespect, so women secretaries and others began fighting against the use of the word 'girl' because it devalued their work and themselves.

The power of words

What is the real power of words? It's the image they give us – what they stand for in our minds. It is important to the way we see ourselves to understand exactly what image is coming across.

Two words can have the same general meaning and still create different images. 'Lady' and 'woman' might be seen to have the same meaning, but they have a different **connotation** (i.e. a sense of what they imply). Another example of this is the words 'bachelor' and 'spinster'. Although they both mean an unmarried person, they certainly imply different things. A bachelor has a positive connotation, while a spinster has a negative one. In this way society uses language to pressurise women into feeling that they should marry – that they are not valuable without a man. But as women gain more power, we find the word 'spinster' is used less often.

Words are not neutral. The exact meaning of words comes from the way they are used in society. **Language** (i.e. using words to communicate thoughts) reflects the values and culture of society. When we look closely at language and what it stands for, we find that it not only reflects our profit-orientated, male-dominated society, but is often used to prop it up and keep women down.

Consciousness raising and language

In consciousness raising groups in the late 1960s and 1970s language was seen as an important issue. As we spoke together about our experiences as women, we began to name the problems that we shared as women. Just being able to use a word like 'sexism' helped us to understand the idea of our oppression. So words played an important part in helping us to understand the concepts behind what we had thought were just individual problems. Communication – speaking about and sharing our experiences – helped us break through a feeling of silence that had individually surrounded us. We saw that we were left out of individual words like 'mankind', which were supposed to stand for all people but only referred to men. We realised that through language and the media we were often characterised in negative, stereotyped ways. From this understanding we came to demand representation.

Changing sexist language

We believed that we could have some control by creating non-sexist language. In the last 25 years feminists have had limited success in fighting against sexist language. Terms such as 'man' or 'mankind' have begun to be seen as not including women equally and are used less often. The point has been made that even if it is claimed that words like 'man' stand for everyone, it still causes people to visualise a male figure, which does not represent women. My favourite example of this is the following sentence: man, as a mammal, breast feeds his young.

Authors of books, especially text books for young people, have been pressured to not use male pronouns like 'he' or 'his' (as if they were neutral) when speaking about general audiences. The use of male terms reflects male power and can be especially harmful to girls and young women who are forming their identities. This is part of the larger problem of sex role stereotyping in children's books, which feminists have been fighting against.

Because of feminist pressure, the 1975 Sex Discrimination Act in Britain caused jobs and their titles to be advertised in a less sexist way. But words like 'milkman' and 'postman' remain in wide general use and I can't believe how often I find women called chairman. Still, there is a wider consciousness now about these terms and about the fact that women object to being excluded or alienated by language.

In the late 1960s women began to call themselves Ms, instead of using Mrs or Miss because these terms defined a woman by her marital status while men, using the universal term Mr, were not being defined by whether or not they were married. While women should not feel pressured into calling themselves Ms, it is encouraging that so many women have decided to redefine themselves in that way. Still, using the title Ms does produce some mixed reactions, depending on the perspective of the person hearing it.

Judging our success

Susan Ehrlich and Ruth King argue that how successful we are at getting non-sexist language used throughout society depends on whether sexist attitudes within society are changing. But even the language used in an anti-sexist campaign can be misappropriated. They cite the example of how during a 'NO MEANS NO' rape awareness campaign sponsored by Queen's University in Kingston, Ontario, Canada, some men put up signs in their dormitory windows such as 'NO MEANS HARDER' and 'STOP MEANS PLEASE'. Two male students held up these signs during a nationally televised hockey game, while a judge in an alleged rape case said that 'no' may mean 'maybe'. These disturbing incidents show how the meaning of the word 'no' is made by society, or **socially constructed**, and how far we still have to go.

But Ehrlich and King do not believe that language reform is useless. Even if it is not completely successful, it does sensitise people to how language treats women unfairly. When people have a choice of which word to use, they are forced to think about it. Over time this can help us all unlearn male-dominated patterns. We also gain power in the process of understanding and changing language. By learning from the problems that come up in that process we know more about what's going on when we are successful in changing sexist language.

Is non-sexist language possible?

As the second wave of feminism developed, some women began to see language as more than an expression of attitudes. They argued that we had to examine the whole relationship between language and thought to understand the way we looked at the world. In other words, the problems of language were more basic. Some feminists felt that language structured the way we looked at things – that through language women see the world from a male point of view.

Man Made Language

Dale Spender's book, *Man Made Language*, did a lot to bring the issue of women and language to the forefront. She argues that language has a determining role in the way we see things and because men control the meaning of language, they can force their way of seeing the world on us.

Spender believes language not only reflects thought but also has an influence on thought. Over time women have been kept from developing forms of thought which express their experiences. Because women's experience is not a part of man-made language women are either **alienated** (i.e. made to feel the outsider) by language, because they have to take on a male point of view, or they are silenced because they cannot communicate since man-made language does not reflect their experience. Dale Spender's ideas tend to reflect a radical feminist position.

A socialist feminist approach

Socialist feminists like Maria Black and Rosalind Coward disagree with Dale Spender because they think her way of viewing power and the meaning of language is too simplistic. Although her work is important because it brings attention to the relationship between language and thought, they feel she looks at this relationship in a misleading way. Seeing language as expressing meanings which are just imposed on women is mistaken, they believe. Other kinds of oppression, like class and race, are intertwined with sexism. Many different forms of oppression are involved in the complex process of power relationships which are seen in the use of language.

Black and Coward see meanings being made possible by language, which structures the experience of individuals.

Feminist linguistic theory

Clearly, there is a strong, important relationship between language and power. Some women have been examining this through the scientific study of language or **linguistics**. A number of them are developing feminist linguistic theories which explore the relationship between women and language.

In *Feminism and Linguistic Theory*, Deborah Cameron calls for a feminist linguistic theory which brings together the issues of language and gender. It would look at the connections between our identity as women and language and also between women's oppression and language. She asks us to think and talk about such questions as: 'What is meant by women's language?' and 'What is the relationship between language and disadvantage?' As far as disadvantage goes, she warns against simply seeing people's problems as coming from the kind of language they use. Although she thinks language is important in keeping women down, she feels that feminist linguistic theory should also take into account other forms of oppression.

EXERCISE 3.2

What do you think about each of the following issues?

1 *Sex differences in language* – Is language used in a different way by women than men? If it is used differently, what does this tell us?
2 *Sexism in language* – How has this changed us? How can we get rid of it?
3 *Alienation* – Do women feel like outsiders in their own language, because it doesn't reflect female experiences? Explain your answer.

———— Literary criticism ————

What is feminist literary criticism?

Feminist literary criticism is looking at literature and authors from a feminist point of view. Coming from an understanding that literature is not neutral but reflects political perspectives, feminist literary criticism is linked to feminist politics. It has needed to be strong and angry, at times, to shake up the certainties of male-dominated culture and make a freer atmosphere for women writers and readers.

Feminist literary critics

Virginia Woolf

In 1929 Virginia Woolf wrote the essay, 'A room of one's own', which is often viewed as the start of modern feminist literary criticism. Not only does she look at the history of women's writing, but she focuses on what historically kept women from writing, examining male social, psychological and material domination. As a talented fiction writer herself, she does this partially through story telling. She creates stories of women being kept out. In one she is excluded from researching the issue of women and fiction at an all-male 'Oxbridge' college library. In another story Shakespeare has a gifted sister, Judith. As a woman, she is excluded both from education and from being an actress in the theatre. Alone in public, it is only her sexuality which is desired and, once pregnant, her burning poet's heart sees no alternative but suicide.

Looking at the reasons behind women's exclusion, Virginia Woolf describes women as a mirror for men, reflecting them at twice their real size. Women need to be kept inferior in order to continue to enlarge men.

Woolf is hopeful about what women can accomplish, saying that Shakespeare's sister lives on in us. What she recommends for women writers is the courage to write what they really think, a room of their own and enough money to be financially independent. In this way she points to the importance of women's material conditions in writing.

As a fiction writer myself, I was touched by Virginia Woolf's ideas. Years back, before Pandora Press decided to publish my novel, with a previous novel still-born after years of effort and with my short stories (as part of a collection with other feminists) being endlessly rejected, I posted this quote about women writing above my desk from the last line of 'A room of one's own': 'To work, even in poverty and obscurity, is worthwhile.'

Simone de Beauvoir

As the second wave of feminism began to break in the late 1960s we found to our great excitement that Simone de Beauvoir had raised many of the issues we were dealing with in her book *The Second Sex*, written in 1949. I remember the thirst with which I read the book, then passed round my discovered treasure to other women, while some of my male, left-wing friends were still laughing at Women's Liberation.

Simone de Beauvoir pointed out that when a woman tries to find her identity she must start by saying, 'I am a woman', while a man doesn't need to do that. Women are forced to define themselves as 'other' (with men being the one) and are separated among men, unable to come together the way other oppressed groups do. Showing how male-dominated culture defines women as inferior she said, 'Legislators, priests, philosophers, writers and scientists have striven to show that the subordinate position of woman is willed in heaven and advantageous on earth.' Those were strong words indeed in 1949, when women in France had only recently been given the vote though they'd played an important role in the underground movement against Nazi occupation during the Second World War, which had only ended a few years earlier. As a novelist and an **existentialist** (i.e. someone who believes that people should be judged by their actions), Simone de Beauvoir called on women themselves, rather than sympathetic men, to determine what were the true possibilities for women. Her ideas can be characterised as socialist feminist.

Kate Millett

When Kate Millett published *Sexual Politics* in 1970 it was like exploding a bomb in an all-male literary club. She used the word 'patriarchy' to talk about the root cause of women's oppression, described sex-role stereotyping and coined the term 'sexual politics' to describe the acting out of dominant and subordinate roles between men and women. Her position can be characterised as that of a radical feminist.

Millett looked at male fiction from the point of view of a woman reader. She told male writers that they could not think of all their readers as men, while encouraging women not to fall into the trap of thinking like a man when reading. Millett focused on the writings of a number of male authors including Norman Mailer (who strongly attacked her in his next book) to expose the male domination shown in sexual descriptions. Millett implied that all men re-created the oppressive sexual politics of the world around them in their fiction. She attacked Freud and tended to discount unconscious psychological factors.

Feminist literary analysis

Socialist feminist analysis

Socialist feminists have argued that not all men write sexist literature and that other factors such as race and class need to be considered. Michèle Barrett criticised Kate Millett's concept of patriarchy because it over-simplified both the different contexts in which women have been oppressed throughout time and the complex relationship between male domination and capitalism.

Barrett has a Marxist feminist analysis of literature. She agrees with the materialist argument that Woolf made when she said that the fact that women and men produce literature under different economic and physical conditions affects the form and content of their work.

Gender stereotyping must not be divided off from its material conditions in history, she believes. Although it's important to have cultural changes, these alone will not end gender stereotyping.

Barrett was concerned about what ideas of gender a reader had when they picked up a book and how these affected the way they interpreted the book. Sexist expectations not only affect how women's and men's writing is read but what is considered 'great literature'. She argued that, in general, a book does not have a fixed meaning; the way it is interpreted depends on the situation and ideas of the reader. Stressing the importance of remembering the fictional nature of literature, she cautioned against 'rampant moralism' – seeing all male authors as sexist and approving of all women writers. But in the end Barrett wanted women to push to have a stronger influence on how they are presented culturally.

Psychoanalytic feminists

Juliet Mitchell challenged Kate Millett's attack on Freud and argued that psychoanalysis played an essential role in understanding patriarchy. She stressed the importance of the unconscious and used the work of Jacques Lacan in her defence of psychoanalysis.

French feminists built on the work of Lacan stressing the symbolic nature of the penis or 'phallus' as representing power and thus seeing male and female differences at a symbolic level, rather than stressing biological differences. Symbols bring us to language, which is seen as a symbol system. Language is the bridge between the inner world of the psyche and the outer world of society. Because language and meaning keep changing, women's relationship to power is a changeable one.

Julia Kristeva

Julia Kristeva, a French-Bulgarian linguist and psychoanalyst, looks at femininity only in terms of its position in the patriarchal symbolic order. The position of femininity is that it is pushed to the edge away from the source of power or **marginalised**. By looking at femininity just in terms of its relationship to patriarchal power she not only sees it as something which can and does change but as something which can include men who are pushed to the margins of the symbolic order (like male avant-garde artists).

As Toril Moi points out, Kristeva argues against a purely biological view of femininity, which sees all women as feminine and all men as masculine and allows the powers of male domination to define all women as marginal both to the symbolic order and to the society as a whole. Politically, Kristeva feels that women still need to demand equality and highlight the difference between the experience of men and women in society to work against sexist oppression; but they must be careful not to get trapped in the patriarchal mindset and take on the very categories of femininity and masculinity set up to limit them. Even if they give new feminist values to the idea of femininity they are still falling into the trap. Kristeva takes on board the ideas of both liberal feminism and radical feminism but wants to move beyond them to a new awareness based on understanding the trap of 'femininity' which patriarchy has set for women. She wants them to see femininity only as a marginalised position in the patriarchal symbolic order rather than taking it on as part of their identity.

Hélène Cixous

Hélène Cixous is another important French theorist with a different view of femininity. She believes femininity is set up as the opposite of masculinity. Masculinity is seen under patriarchy as being powerful, while femininity is seen in a negative way as being powerless.

She calls on women to move beyond **binary thought** (seeing opposites where only one can be positive or powerful) where the male side always wins under patriarchy. She wants what she calls a 'free play of meaning' in which words don't get their meaning from the limited, closed circle of male and female opposites. She doesn't believe that meaning has to stay as it is. Instead Cixous wants to call 'woman' powerful and full of energy – to see the female as where life comes from and to create a feminine language which works against the patriarchal division of opposites in which the female side is always the loser. In the English-speaking world we can see an example of this in the way the radical feminist Mary Daly has redefined the meaning of the word 'crone' (which from the point of view of male-dominated language had the negative meaning of an old, meddling woman) to refer to a wise and powerful older woman.

Cixous calls on women to put their bodies into their writing – by freeing themselves of guilt and openly, joyfully using their sexuality in their writing. She encourages women to imagine the possibility of a language in which they can truly express themselves. Other feminists have pointed to the problem of how well this language would be understood, but the focus for Cixous is on freeing women to be creative beyond the limiting force of patriarchy.

EXERCISE 3.3

1 Think about the different views of femininity which have been presented above. Do you agree with any of them? If so, in what ways? In what ways do you disagree?
2 What is your view of femininity in language and literature? How do you see the idea of femininity being used in language and literature today? How would you like it to be used?

Black feminists

Barbara Smith argues that the main task of Black feminist criticism should be to look at the ways in which being Black and female have played a major role in the writings of Black women. She points out that Black women writers have a specific literary tradition. As far as themes, style and concepts are concerned, Black women writers have common ways of producing literature which come out of their shared social, economic and political experiences. These experiences and Black female language have been used by Black women to create a rich literature which goes beyond white/male structures. She advises the Black feminist critic to use her own ideas and ways of looking at literature rather than be bound by white/male literary thought and to let her writing come out of her own identity. She sees Black feminist literary criticism coming out of and contributing to the Black feminist movement.

Alice Walker talks about the history of Black women artists in the United States. These women were rich in spirituality, the basis of art, yet they were not allowed any release for their creativity. She marvels at how the creativity of Black women was kept alive when it was a crime to read or write and they were not allowed the freedom of other arts. Yet they kept alive the idea of creative expression. Phillis Wheatley (a slave in the 1700s) became a poet, Black women created beautiful quilts and sang. And, over time, there were Black women writers like the anthropologist Zora Neale Hurston. Alice Walker celebrates the creativity of ordinary Black women like her mother who worked from dawn until late at night but still created a beautiful garden with brilliant colours and original designs wherever she lived.

The Black heroine

In her introduction to *Black Women Writers at Work* Claudia Tate points out the major role of the Black heroine in the literature of modern Black women writers in the United States. The Black heroine is usually not going on a physical journey in which she is travelling because she has children to take care of and is tied to a small area. There she is involved in her community with friends and relatives. Her journey then is an inner one – a journey of self-discovery. This involves having deep relationships with other people. These relationships are either the kind where the heroine is troubled or confused or, after she has gained some understanding of herself and other people, where she and others are helpful to each other.

The Black heroine must often nurture her own self-esteem. She must deal with the double burden of racism and sexism in such a way as to survive with dignity. She struggles against her oppression both as a Black person and a woman with an inner courage and self-confidence which echoes in the lives of other Black women. She lives life as a process and often the resolution of that process involves change, which takes one of two forms. Either the heroine makes a conscious decision to change and acts on it, or there is an inner change. This inner change is based on an understanding that although she can't alter the situation, she is able to move beyond former boundaries because she sees where they are and uses her intellectual and emotional powers to build a meaningful life in a difficult situation. Through an intense inner process, the Black heroine develops a sense of clarity about herself and her relationship to others and about the world around her.

Lesbian feminists

Lesbian critics have studied the lives and works of lesbian authors from Gertrude Stein to Audre Lorde to look at both the variety of lesbian experiences and the unifying factors in life and literature.

They have also examined the past experiences of other women writers in a new light. Writing in the Lesbian History Group's *Not a Passing Phase* Sheila Jeffreys points to evidence which shows that in countries like the United States and Britain, passionate friendships between middle-class women in the eighteenth and nineteenth centuries were socially acceptable and a crucial part of a number of women's lives. This could involve everything from kisses and passionate embraces to declarations of love and cuddles or intimacies in a shared bed for a night. It was only in the late nineteenth century, with the ever-growing strength of the women's movement, that these passionate friendships between women threatened male power and became socially unacceptable. Then this level of emotional and physical intimacy became classified as lesbianism. Of course, the other part of what is generally considered lesbianism today involves genital contact. But Jeffreys argues that in studying women's history we must be flexible and not impose our present values and definitions onto women who lived under such different conditions. She does not believe it is necessary for women to have had genital sex or to have been a part of a recognisable lesbian subculture for them to be seen as having had a relationship to lesbianism.

Elaine Miller of the Lesbian History Group provides an example of these ideas when she argues that Charlotte Brontë was in love with Ellen Nussey for most of her life in a way that should be described as lesbian. She bases this on the 500 letters Brontë sent to Nussey (which Vita Sackville-West described as love letters that left little doubt about Brontë's tendencies) and their close, passionate friendship which involved them staying together for weeks at a time, sharing a bed at times. But Miller does not see this as creating a contradiction between Brontë's life and work. In other words, there wasn't a basic contradiction between the kind of heterosexual romantic novels she wrote and her loving relationship with a woman, Ellen Nussey.

The works of a number of Black lesbian writers have also been examined in a new light by critics like Barbara Smith.

Feminist literary criticism and difference

Just as feminist literary criticism, in general, looks at literature and authors from a female point of view, our differences means that, for example, Irish women, women with disabilities and/or working-class women will look at literature and authors from the point of view of their other identities and oppressions, as well as from the viewpoint of being a woman. This process can be helpful to all of us as it heightens our awareness about how characters are portrayed, how structures of writing are defined, how language is used and the specific forms of oppression of different women writers.

There are varying opinions about how this process of looking at literature through our differences should take place. For example, Maggie Humm argues that the writing of Black women and lesbians have features which are common to both and which differ from a general white feminism. She sees both as having their own distinct literary traditions which have helped to create their culture. And because of their position as outsiders, lesbian and Black women authors have each played a primarily political role, seeing the link between artistic creation and political realities. She asks how they can be looked at separately when a number of important Black women writers are lesbians.

Maggie Humm argues against Black and lesbian criticism being used in an exclusively separatist way, emphasising that both perspectives have an essential role to play within feminist criticism. This brings us back to the question of whether our differences should be used in an exclusive way or to develop awareness by a particular group of women which is then available to be shared by all women, taking into account that this must be done in a respectful, sensitive manner by the larger group. This issue involves the fact that women often fit into a number of categories of oppression.

Tillie Olsen's *Silences*

Tillie Olsen's classic book *Silences* speaks both about women's differences and about how women in general have been silenced. She collected her talks and writings from the 1960s and the early 1970s into a book which came out in 1978. It looks at how women's household responsibilities and their traditional training to put the needs of others before their own needs has either kept them from having the time and focus to write or has meant that they couldn't devote themselves fully to their writing.

Expressing the heartfelt experiences of a working-class woman writer who had suffered unnatural silences brought on by the restrictions of society, Tillie Olsen not only tells it like it is but also documents her thesis that those who are not privileged by society because of their sex, class and/or race are obstructed and silenced. This inequality of circumstance means that only one out of twelve women writers survives. As a 'survivor' Tillie Olsen wanted to bear witness for those who could not. She showed how women's experience and literature were devalued throughout the ages and how women writers were not taken seriously or even taken into consideration by most men writers, critics or academics who decided what was 'great' literature. She also wrote about how much of women's literature was dropped from history as books went out of print.

A personal view of feminist literary criticism

As a feminist novelist and short-story writer, talking about feminist literary criticism is not something which I can just do from an external point of view. It's also a part of my life. Perhaps my tale of the inner workings of a woman writer will give you insight into feminist literature.

I once met Tillie Olsen at a Writers' Union fund-raising event in San Francisco. There I was, a young unknown writer. Just as she was leaving I got up the courage to go to her and tell her how much her writing meant to me. Tillie Olsen opened her arms and hugged me.

I feel like one of her privileged survivors, though I don't come from what would be considered a privileged background. So what were the privileges that allowed me to end up among the one in twelve women who survived the process to write?

Deep-seated defiance   This has its base in a thrust for justice that emanated from the lesson of the Holocaust for a Jew who grew up believing that those who watch genocide and do nothing bear responsibility. It was developed through the Civil Rights movement and the anti-Vietnam War movement in the United States and was refined to new personal heights through the Women's Liberation Movement, especially the London Chalk Farm Women's Consciousness Raising Group in Britain.

Obsession   I tried to give up writing many times when rejection of my work ripped at my heart. But I soon found that silence drove me crazy.

My Mother   Her love has given me such power and her example helped me to believe in myself. She was deeply spiritual while valuing education, along with plain speaking and common sense.

Luck   I managed to find ways of supporting myself which gave me some time to write.

Support   I've spent over 25 years living with a man who took half the responsibility for our children and the household. Not only that, but he believed in me.

Community (at times)   Demonstrations usually inspired me and I often found power in meeting with other women.

Responsibility   Understanding how privileged I was made me feel that I had to speak for all those women throughout the world and throughout time who were silenced. Here is an excerpt from one of my short stories, 'Mummy needs to work':

> I remember Granny telling stories round the kitchen table while she cooked. Her words conjured up worlds I'd never known. They taught me fortitude and made me cry.
>
> The one about how her mother died in childbirth sticks with me the most. She said her mother used to make up poems and try to have her memorise them, so they wouldn't be forgotten. I wanted to hear the poems, but she couldn't remember. How could they be gone? I longed for those poems and used to try and make them up myself.
>
> I need your poems Great Grandmother. I need their courage and strength. And you need me to speak for you. Is that what possesses me to write?
>
> But I don't know your poems. I can only tell my own story. Still, I can become what you were never allowed to be, a writer.'

EXERCISE 3.4

1 What does looking at literature from a woman's point of view mean to you? How does it make you feel about writing?
2 Which feminist literary analysis do you agree with most? Why do you feel closest to that one?
3 Which feminist literary analysis do you disagree with most? Explain your reasons. Try to include arguments from other literary critics.

4
WOMEN'S LITERATURE

Feminist literature is a glowing charge of emotional truth. The flow of imagination washing over the hard, cold 'facts', used against us. The essence of ourselves. A spirit to sustain us. Feminist literature is the energy from our safe heart harnessed so we can speak and hear our own truth.

A limited survey of women's literature

With such a wide vista of women's written creativity before me and so little space to write about it, I've had to limit my focus. I have chosen to concentrate on the example of women novelists who wrote in England, although they may have come from other places. I know this means leaving out women in other countries and areas of Britain, as well as other forms of expression like poetry and play writing. But perhaps my brief survey will encourage you to look beyond its limits to the wider picture. I will suggest the names of some women writers from other places near the end of the chapter.

Women novelists before 1840

Although it's impossible to know exactly when English women started being published, from about 1750 their books began to be seen in print, mostly as novels. Because of women's limited role in society (see Chapter 2) many early female authors felt uncomfortable about having a professional identity and some even published without using a name at all.

Almost all the women authors until the end of the nineteenth century came from the same social group – upper-middle-class, aristocratic or professional families. Hard as it was for them, the class system and other forms of social oppression made it nearly impossible for the vast majority of women in England to come into print. Still, we must remember that these women expressed themselves creatively in many forms.

Grace Agular

Of course, there were exceptions to the picture I've just painted. One such woman was Grace Agular. She was a Jewish woman writer in England, whose ancestors had fled the Spanish Inquisition. Between 1835 and her early death in 1847 she wrote poetry and popular novels about women's domestic life. She was also credited with being the first woman to try to educate the British public about Judaism and Jewish women through her non-fiction books. Some of her novels went into as many as 30 editions, long after her death. Yet today she has been almost completely forgotten.

Women writers from 1840–1880

In *A Literature Of Their Own,* Elaine Showalter sets out to reclaim English women's literature. In order to develop a clear understanding of English women authors and their novels she looked at the few women, over a period of history, who were seen by the literary establishment as 'great' – Jane Austen, the Brontës, Mary Anne Evans (who wrote under the male **pseudonym** of George Eliot) and Virginia Woolf – alongside the other women novelists of their times. These other novelists were often extremely popular but were dropped from literary history. This follows the same pattern of silencing that we saw in women's history in general. By looking at women authors in their literary, social and historical context, Showalter was able to suggest three different phases for English women novelists.

To show the development of women's writing Showalter begins her study with those novelists from the time when women authors used male pseudonyms in the 1840s to George Eliot's death in 1880. This was basically a time when women tried to imitate dominant male traditions and internalised their standards of art and social roles. In other words, a time when women were trying to prove themselves.

Three generations

The first generation of women writers in this period were born between 1800 and 1820 and began publishing fiction in the 1840s. The Brontë sisters, Elizabeth Barrett Browning, Mrs Gaskell, Harriet Martineau and George Eliot were all of this generation and were the women identified with the Golden Age of Victorian Female Authors. This generation was breaking new ground; in other fields it included women like Florence Nightingale of nursing fame and Mary Carpenter who did much for schools for poor children. The second generation, which was born between 1820 and 1840, built on the gains of the women before them but were seen to have less of a sense of originality and dedication. They included Charlotte Yonge, Dinah Mulock Craik, Margaret Oliphant and Elizabeth Lynn Linton. The third generation was born between 1840 and 1860. Their writing broadened into sensationalist novels and children's books, while their types of work expanded into editorial and publishing jobs. They were able to be more businesslike and unconventional, as well as efficient and productive, because they were much better at dealing with their dual roles as women and professional writers.

Conflict between traditional role and being a writer

The conflict between a traditional woman's role, focusing on the needs of others, and the role of a professional writer, which is self-centred because it puts one's own development and fulfilment first, is something that we still deal with today. For Victorian women writers that balancing act was much more difficult. It meant they had to overcome their guilt about writing while proving themselves in the domestic sphere. This led talented writers like Charlotte Brontë to sincerely work at ending her desire to write and, when that failed, to keep those around her from seeing what she was doing.

Some women were able to justify their writing because of a need to earn money. Working in publishing (also as readers and copy-editors) was almost the only profession, other than teaching, open to nineteenth-century middle-class women. About half of women writers born in the nineteenth-century were unmarried; others married late or needed to earn money because their husbands died, were ill or had financial problems. Of the married ones, 65 per cent had children, though they tended to have fewer than the norm of six. The double burden of providing domestic and financial support could affect the quality of a woman's fiction as Virginia Woolf points out in *Three*

Guineas, using the example of Mrs Oliphant, who was the sole support of her children. But for most women the lack of alternatives focused their involvement on literature and, if they were published, allowed them to branch out into journalism.

Lack of formal education

Lack of formal education was a strong barrier for all women in the nineteenth century. Women novelists of the 1840 to 1880 period envied the classical education which they were denied. First-generation novelists from this period had to have an amazing amount of drive and self-control to educate themselves since they were not, in general, given a formal education in school, as men of their class were. The inferior status of the Victorian, middle-class girl was dramatically brought home when her brother left for school. We see this in novels such as George Eliot's *The Mill on the Floss*.

Although almost all women writers were self-taught, they were expected to have the same level of scholarship in their novels as men. Male critics gleefully pounced on any errors they made, though they claimed to be more lenient with women.

The double standard

Because of a double standard in the judging of literature, women writers were continually running on a treadmill, unable to reach equality. They were seen first as women and only secondly as writers. A number of novelists from this period felt the need to use a male pseudonym to get published as well as to get fairer treatment from critics, and sometimes to protect themselves from their own families or friends.

Male and female categories

Male and female categories of writing were strictly divided. Reviewers saw women writers as having refinement and high moral tone; their special areas were supposed to be sentiment, tact and the ability to observe plus knowledge about a woman's character and domestic life. But they were seen to lack abstract intelligence and education, originality and humour plus self-control and knowledge about men's character. Men writers were seen far more positively as having everything from intelligence and knowledge of everyone's character (because of their wide experience) to humour and open mindedness and from clarity and shrewdness to power and self-control.

WHATEVER IS SHE DOING IN THERE?

Until about 1875, the double literary standard was so taken for granted that reviewers would look at anonymous novels or those with possible pseudonyms and use the categories I've just mentioned to say if the author was male or female. As you might have guessed, they were often wrong. For example, after *Adam Bede* was published most reviewers thought George Eliot was a clerical gentleman. She had already put herself in conflict with Victorian values by living with a man outside marriage; imagine the hostility when she revealed her female authorship of this respected book! The *Saturday Review* told its readers that *Adam Bede* had been thought to be too good to be a woman's story. But Barbara Bodichon, a radical feminist, who had said the book was written by a woman all along, was joyful.

Supposed inferiority

The powerful belief that female bodies were inferior weighed women writers down. Many Victorian's prejudices about the inferiority of women were linked to their now thoroughly disproved theories about other races and women having smaller brains which were less efficient. Although many scientists of the day supported these theories, women doctors like Alice Putman Jacobi argued against them. Clearly, these theories were used to justify a hierarchy that kept men of the dominant group in power while excluding all other people on the basis of their race, gender and/or class.

The limits on women's experiences were used as another reason to see their literature as inferior. Critics agreed that the novel was the proper place for women, if they had to write, since it allowed them their focus on psychological motivation as well as using their powers of observation.

Many women novelists of this period reacted to the construction of their inferiority not with anger but by trying to show that they were domestically oriented and that their writing came out of their feminine role, adding to it rather than taking away from it. Although the Brontës answered criticism based on their sex head-on, George Eliot was the only one to talk about the relationship between women's experience and the actual structure and content of the novel.

The first generation

By the 1840s women's novels had been established as a way of looking at how females influenced those around them both domestically and in their social circle, reinforcing the idea that this was a middle-class woman's proper sphere.

Female models

Women novelists of this first generation looked for models for their own work. Unlike men, who could study their long literary history at university or meet in coffee houses, women were highly restricted and isolated. Jane Austen, who was of an earlier generation having written from 1790 until her death in 1817, was a favourite model recommended by male critics. But novelists like Charlotte Brontë found her too restrained. Instead the French writer Amantine Dupin – better known as George Sand – with her rebellious life style and passionate novels was seen as more inspiring. A dozen of her novels were translated into English in the 1840s.

Critics set up a narrow division between Austen and Sand and saw early women novelists as coming from one trend or the other. Charlotte Brontë identified with Sand because her spontaneous literature came from a woman's body as well as her heart and because she was romantic and able to express her feelings. But George Eliot was seen as coming from the Austen trend as a writer who was intellectual and cultured.

By 1860, with their increased popularity, Brontë and Eliot were set up as the models to which all other women writers were compared by the critics. In this way women novelists were kept competing with each other in a limited women's sphere.

Changes from 1860

There were major changes for women in the 1860s. The market for women's literature grew, along with opportunities for women publishers and editors, as well as actual printers. For the first time women created feminist presses which meant they not only had business and editorial control, but were also able to train and hire women as printers. In 1860 Emily Faithful started the Victoria Printing Press which published many of the women's journals and magazines which dealt with issues such as women and work and suffrage. Women saw the value in using journalism to give them a voice in politics, as they were excluded from it in so many other ways (see Chapter 2).

Sensationalist women writers

Women were gaining more independence both in the publishing industry and in their style of writing. The new sensationalist women writers like Mary E. Braddon, Charlotte Riddell, Amelia B. Edwards, Florence Marryat, Helen Reeves and Rhoda Broughton valued passion and assertiveness in their literature, seeing themselves following the trend of Charlotte Brontë instead of George Eliot. But their heroines could actually achieve some independence, as the sensationalist authors built on and developed the discontent of their ever-growing middle-class female readers who were feeling increasingly trapped in their role at home within the traditional family.

Mary Braddon was a popular female sensationalist whose novels were serialised in the new magazines, which further expanded her audience. In a novel like her *Lady Audley's Secret* we see how female sensationalists not only overturned the sex roles stereotypes of male sensationalist writing (making the heroine the dangerous, active player) but also used delicate, domesticated women characters to play the part of the discontented wife capable of murder. Strikingly, Braddon turned around the threat of women being locked away as mad for not staying within the Victorian feminine role by implying that if middle- class women were trapped in the home and not given access to careers, they might well take out their frustrations on their families in murderous ways.

EXERCISE 4.1

What do you think about English women novelists from 1840–80?

1 What held them back the most?
2 What was their main contribution?
3 Which novelist do you like best? Why?

Feminist writers

In *Border Traffic*, Maggie Humm argues that, although not all women's fiction is feminist, we can define feminist women writers in a broad way. This wide definition includes woman authors who were asking different kinds of questions about the way women are socialised, those who were moving beyond the limits set by the literary establishment by representing women in a positive way and/or those who were presenting female topics in such a way as to attack the social and economic inequalities facing women. In other words, she argues that, in work which focuses on women's issues in order to look at gender and socio-economic inequalities, and which tries to give us insights into how these might be improved, we can see a broadly defined feminist consciousness.

Feminist trends

Using this broad definition I have divided feminist writers into different trends. Although I'll give general dates for these trends, clearly the work of some writers overlaps these dates, just as their work changes during their life times.

From about 1880–1919 (right after the first, limited vote was won) there was the suffragist trend. This includes writers such as Olive Schreiner, Sarah Grand and Elizabeth Robins. During this period women writers were openly protesting against dominant male standards and values and fighting for their own rights and values.

In the 1920s there was the aesthetic trend which includes Rebecca West, Virginia Woolf, Radcliff Hall and Dorothy Richardson.

Aesthetics is the study of art and beauty. In this period feminist ideas were applied to language itself and to a woman's view of beauty through literature.

In the 1930s we have the left-wing trend including Vera Brittain, Winifred Holtby, Storm Jameson and Sylvia Townsend Warner.

In the 1960s we have the pre-second-wave trend including Margaret Drabble, Nell Dunn, Doris Lessing and Jean Rhys. They focused on issues which would become major concerns for second-wave feminists.

From the 1970s to the present we have the second wave trend with its diversity and expansion of feminist writing and the development of feminist presses.

Suffragist trend

After 1880 women moved beyond novels of escape and domestic murder to those about the politics that they were being progressively drawn into. In the 1880s and 1890s women writers played a major role in forming and popularising feminist ideas. Just as women's novels from 1840–80 had focused on domestic realism, feminist literature was about protest. Authors like Sarah Grand saw suffrage and the issues surrounding it as a better strategy for women than self-sacrifice.

Suffragist feminist writers had a sense of sisterhood and idealism, wanting to expose society's evils and use a specifically female influence to determine how things ought to be. Women began to feel they had a moral right to take leadership especially in relation to issues like the Contagious Disease Acts campaign (1864–84). Through this campaign horrifying stories came out about how women prostitutes, or those accused of prostitution, were being brutally treated in Lock Hospitals, while men were neither being examined nor punished for their part. (The original Lock Hospital was in London; the name was also applied to other hospitals which treated the same illnesses – venereal diseases.)

Exposés on child prostitution, Jack the Ripper's unsolved murders of women and the fact that venereal disease could be passed on to women and their children led women to demand sexual self-control from men. Involvement in campaigns against sexual exploitation meant women writers were able to begin to use the sexual vocabulary which had been reserved for men. Suffragist feminist literature reacted against male sexual force in the bedroom and the outside world. Rather than more sexual licence for women, it tended to focus on maternal love. This even led to fantasy stories of virgin births and societies ruled by women.

Why aren't suffragist novelists considered 'great'?

None of the suffragist feminist novelists have been considered 'great' women writers by male-dominated literary history. They were seen, even at the time, as more focused on ideas than on pure art. But doesn't any work of art reflect some set of values and ideas? In countries like Britain these have too often been male-dominated, profit- orientated ideas. Even if the suffragist novelists did focus on their cause, that doesn't, in itself, lower the quality of their work. But it could well affect the judgement of those threatened by their cause or critics who don't see their work as being within the boundaries of what they define as 'great'. After all, what is seen as 'great' is a judgement which reflects the values of those with the power to set the standards. I'm not saying there shouldn't be standards for literature. But these standards must be questioned and examined. Clearly, in a male-dominated, profit-orientated society these standards are not completely neutral.

Exceptions to the elite mould

In the suffragist feminist novelists we find exceptions to the mould of elite, English backgrounds for nineteenth century women writers. In fact, two of the best known writers of this time grew up in deprived circumstances outside England. Olive Schreiner was born and brought up in poverty on a series of missionary stations in South Africa. And Sarah Grand, the pseudonym of Frances Clarke McFall, had a deprived childhood in Ireland and Northern England. Clearly their early life experiences not only influenced their writing but how they saw the world.

Olive Schreiner

Olive Schreiner was a feminist, a socialist and a supporter of justice for Black people. As Ruth First and Ann Scott point out in *Olive Schreiner: a Biography*, her complexity and contradictions meant that critics could pull apart the different aspects of her work (and her life) and use one part to discredit another. *The Story of An African Farm*, her first successful novel which she published in England under the pseudonym Ralph Iron, shows her use of strong female symbolism (for example a ring) as well as her deep understanding of women's suffering and feminist ideas. In Lyndall she created the first completely serious feminist heroine in an English novel. Schreiner's ill health and emotional conflicts made sustained, productive writing difficult. But she did publish stories with hidden or symbolic meanings – **allegories** – which she called *Dreams*. After her death the novel she'd been writing and rewriting for years was published.

Schreiner had a strong, inspirational influence on the feminist movement. Her *Dreams* were read aloud by suffragettes in Holloway prison and her non-fiction work, *Women and Labour* was seen as the bible of the movement. Although she was caught between her own oppression as a woman and the pressures of trying to conceptualise new social and economic possibilities, Schreiner inspired other women writers such as Virginia Woolf and Doris Lessing.

Sarah Grand

Sarah Grand did not come from a culture of women writing, but left her husband and created a new identity for herself from her own force of will. She became a highly successful novelist and in 1893 her stylish, original novel *The Heavenly Twins* sold 20,000 copies in the first week alone. The talk of the town, raising strong feelings for and against, it was about a woman's right to independence, sex-role stereotyping and even dealt with venereal disease.

Her later semi-autobiographical novel, *The Beth Book*, looks at the heroine Beth's difficult childhood in Ireland, her disastrous marriage to a Lock Hospital doctor of prostitutes and finally her development into a feminist writer. Grand uses the symbolic fantasy device of Beth finding a secret room in which she can have a private space to escape her economic and educational disadvantages and dedicate herself to the literary purpose of writing for women instead of men. Beth feels that women focus on the important problems of life and struggle to make life beautiful, while men merely amuse one another with thoughts on Art and Style. In the end Beth publishes anonymously and even the male establishment has to give her credit.

Sarah Grand is an example of an extremely popular woman writer who has been thoroughly excluded from male-dominated literary history. Clearly, there is a link between her exclusion and her politics and background. As well as writing, Grand was an active member of the feminist movement both in the Women Writers Suffrage League and later as president of the Tunbridge Wells branch of the National Union of Women's Suffrage Societies. After women gained the vote she was the honorary Mayor of Bath.

Elizabeth Robins and Votes for Women

By 1906 the suffrage campaign had reached such a high level of intensity and public awareness that women couldn't help thinking about it, no matter what their beliefs. That year Elizabeth Robins wrote a play called *Votes for Women*, which she then turned into a novel. Both the play and novel, *The Convert* (1907), proved to be not only popular but highly influential. Robins gives a realistic account of what it was like to be a suffragette, suggesting that these women were being brutally handled in a way that had sexual overtones. She uses the term 'sex-antagonism' to describe the anger between men and women. Because the suffragettes recognised sex-antagonism they were free to act while other women used up their energy suppressing their anger. She also went into the unexplored territory of women's psychology, feeling that the suffrage movement needed to raise the consciousness of middle-class women.

In 1908 Robins became the president of the newly-formed Women Writers Suffrage League. Here we see professional women writers understanding the power in coming together for feminist aims. They wrote plays and novels as well as letters, essays and newspaper articles calling for the vote. Robins linked women writers with the working class, each needing to turn out products for those in power, focusing on the fact that women were dependent on male publishers.

'Freewomen'

As well as women writers opposed to feminism, who were in the Anti-Suffrage League called Antis, there were those who had a different perspective on feminism. These women wrote for *Freewoman* magazine, attacked the narrow focus on the vote as the way to free women and developed their own ideas on free love and individualism. Rebecca West came out against Christabel Pankhurst's view that, in the end, male lust was the basis of woman's oppression. Later West wrote her own feminist novels.

Overall, suffragist feminist novelists showed the importance of culture in bringing about political change. In doing so they took on a different role – moving beyond the privacy of writing into the difficulties and rewards of collectivism.

EXERCISE 4.2

How do you view Suffragist Feminist novelists?

1 How did Suffragist Feminist novelists help women gain the vote?
2 Which author were you most interested in? Why?
3 How do you think 'great' literature should be defined and decided upon?

Aesthetic trend

By 1920 women had not only lived through the First World War but had won the vote for many women over 30. Many activists, although not all, had switched their energies from suffrage to the war effort, using it as a way to prove women worthy of the vote. The war itself had been so brutal – with so many people maimed and killed, along with soldiers returning home 'shell shocked' with emotional traumas. Women writers reacted to the violence of the war by turning away – turning inward. But they did not turn inward in an individual way with a writing style which was very personal. Feeling that they had come into their own as women, they explored the beauty in literature from a female point of view. Their interest was in developing the truly female art of literature. In their novels we can see new images of women's feelings. Although their main focus was not on how their literature would affect politics, we find feminist ideas in their fiction as well as in their non-fiction.

Feminist pacifism and the unconscious

Virginia Woolf and Rebecca West both show a feminist pacifism and look at issues of violence and sexuality in relationship to the unconscious. We see this in novels like *Mrs Dalloway* (1925) by Woolf and *The Return of the Soldier* (1918) by West. Both books have a shell-shocked soldier who is a symbol of the bankruptcy of male imperialist power. Woolf uses him to describe her own negative experiences of the 'rest cure' for madness, which was so often used on women. In linking the experience of the shell-shocked soldier with Mrs Dalloway, Woolf shows the harm of suppressing emotions and how this isolates women. West shows how women in middle-class society can find themselves being **parasitic women** (i.e. living off and needing to maintain patriarchy) while she also demonstrates the power in women working together. Both novelists go beyond established boundaries by deeply involving their readers in looking at the meaning of history and psychology, while examining strong women's friendships. They also wrote feminist non-fiction, which discussed a wide variety of issues.

Beyond heterosexuality

In 1928 feminist novelists moved beyond heterosexuality in their writing. In *Orlando*, Woolf used **androgyny** (being both female and male) to look at issues of gender and class in a new way. And in *The Well of Loneliness*, Radclyffe Hall created the first full-length novel which looked at lesbianism sympathetically. As Rosalind Miles points out in *The Female Form*, Hall's semi-autobiographical novel was written because she felt that the love of women had never been the serious focus of fiction before. In the novel there is a sense of an honest desire to tell the truth about women's love and force the society to face lesbianism. This was a brave act, especially for a woman who was herself vulnerable as a lesbian, and one for which Hall paid dearly. She was persecuted through the courts for obscenity and eventually driven out of the country as an enemy of the family and the state. She suffered this because she told about the pain of lesbian women in a society which would not recognise their right to exist.

Feminist culture through language

Happy endings for women were in short supply in the novels of the aesthetic trend. These authors focused more on feminist culture in language and psychology than on society. Aesthetic novelists were better able to look at feminist issues through their fiction than they were to point to solutions. This is clear in the work of Dorothy M. Richardson.

Richardson believed there were specific qualities, based on being male or female, which came out in the way a person wrote rather than just in what they said. She saw language as being constructed by men and used differently by women. Although she felt women were at a disadvantage using words and meanings made by men, she believed women communicated at a higher level. Richardson created a fluid style of writing, presenting what she saw as the many associations which were held at the same time in the female way of seeing things. Virginia Woolf believed her unconventional sentence structure could be useful in describing a woman's mind.

Left-wing trend

In the 1930s, left-wing feminists moved the agenda back to social issues. They were concerned about the welfare of many different women including those in the working class and women of different races.

Vera Brittain and Winifred Holtby

Vera Brittain and Winifred Holtby drew on the theories of Olive Schreiner with Brittain focusing on linking the private and public experiences of women and Holtby pointing out that if people are considered inferior because of their sex or their race, limiting their opportunities, the progress of the entire society was in danger. They were both concerned about working mothers and motherhood in general, as well as women in the labour force. Because there was a 'marriage bar' on women wanting professional jobs after the First World War, women might have to choose between marriage and a career. But in her novel *Honourable Estate* (1936), Brittain argues for a new kind of marriage of equal partnership. She actually had such a marriage – keeping her own name, having children while she continued to work and maintaining her strong friendship with Holtby.

Storm Jameson and Sylvia Townsend Warner

Storm Jameson and Sylvia Townsend Warner both examined issues of class and feminism in their work. Often their novels focused on the heroine coming to understand that to find herself she has to break through the boundaries of male domination and class. *None Turn Back* by Jameson and *Summer Will Show* by Townsend Warner, both published in 1936, are socialist novels in that they show how women change dramatically by having radical political experiences. But the way they change is specifically feminist. It is sharing love for children and one another, not just the general political comradeship, which transforms them. Both point to the fact that society wouldn't acknowledge the strengths of independent women or the struggles of those who are seen as outcasts.

Major political events are used to explore women's experiences of growth. In *None Turn Back*, Jameson uses the General Strike of 1926 to talk about sexual politics and a specifically female crossing of the class divide. In *Summer Will Show* Townsend Warner, a lesbian communist, uses the Paris Commune of 1848 to discuss the rejection of **bourgeois** (middle and upper class) values by women who raise their consciousness and develop their own identity. In the novel this includes the heroine's empowering experience of lesbianism and a vision of the possibility of a society which is free of gender, class and race limitations.

EXERCISE 4.3

How would you compare the aesthetic trend with the left-wing trend?

1 How are the two trends different? What are the main differences between them?
2 What do they have in common? In what ways are they similar?
3 Which author did you find most interesting from these two trends? Why?

Pre-second-wave trend

In the early and mid 1960s women novelists raised issues which later became important concerns for second wave feminists. Margaret Drabble and Nell Dunn focused on the experience of single motherhood, Doris Lessing's *The Golden Notebook* (1962) introduced women striving toward modern feminism and Jean Rhys examined issues of race and colonialism.

Single motherhood

In looking at motherhood outside the traditional family and marriage, Drabble in *The Millstone* (1965) and Dunn in *Poor Cow* (1967) not only examine the positive and negative elements for women of raising children on their own, but also argue that traditional marriage itself deforms women's experience of having children. In *The Millstone* the heroine shares experiences across class boundaries, through the NHS, and develops a deeper understanding of herself through being with young children. *Poor Cow* examines single motherhood in the working class with a heroine who is able to use openly sexual language and look at the physically pleasurable side of motherhood. It also raises the issue of wife battering.

Doris Lessing's The Golden Notebook

I remember the wonder and excitement I felt when my women friends and I 'discovered' Doris Lessing's *The Golden Notebook*. In the late 1960s when it seemed to us that we were entering the completely new territory of Women's Liberation we found, in *The Golden Notebook*, models of women which touched us and echoed inside. As a South African ex-patriot, a left-wing activist and a writer who put women at the emotional centre of her fiction, Lessing was able to bring an outsider's depth of vision to British culture. At the same time she dealt with women raising their consciousness – from having a distinctly female way of thinking and using language to coming to a greater understanding of themselves. The novel is divided into various notebooks which each tell about different aspects of the heroine's life. Yet the book itself is about how life cannot be divided off into neat compartments. Breaking down society's division between private and public, the heroine writes about things like deciding to leave the Communist Party while at the same time talking about her own menstruation. It's the heroine's acceptance of the different aspects of herself which allows her to finish writing the golden notebook.

Jean Rhys on colonialism and racism

In *Wide Sargasso Sea* (1966) Jean Rhys shows how colonialism is racist and patriarchal. She presents a positive vision of Black and **Creole** (either a white person born in the Caribbean or a person who has a Black parent and a white parent) women, while looking at the issue of women and difference. Her novel sets out to retell the story of Bertha Rochester in *Jane Eyre*. Rhys calls Bertha Antoinette and uses her novel to look at how different women were marginalised in the 1830s and 1840s. The power of Black women is celebrated in Christophine who not only makes and tells Antoinette's history but also ably uses and translates between various dialects and languages. Black, Creole and white working-class women are all given an authentic voice. Being clear about their differences Rhys, who was a white Creole, was able to show the bonds between women. By reinterpreting history and the characters in Brontë's novel from the viewpoint of the 1960s, Rhys took a fresh look at issues of race, gender and colonialism.

Second-wave trend

From about 1970 to the present we have the trend of second-wave feminism with its wide variety of authors and **genres** or kinds of writing, its link to the feminist movement and the development of feminist presses. Although there's been an important influence by

American writers in this era I will keep my literary focus on women's writing in Britain. With the vast number of recent novelists I'll just choose a few to serve as examples of different aspects of the second-wave trend. But first I must set the scene.

Feminist presses and the movement

The reblossoming of feminism was a freeing force for women writers. This political movement, which was about women finding themselves and their independence, encouraged us to take matters into our own hands. An important part of this was the development of feminist presses such as Virago, The Women's Press, Pandora and Sheba. Not only did Virago bring important novelists from other eras back into print to give us a sense of continuity, but feminist presses encouraged women to believe in their own explorations by creating the possibility for them to be published without having to tailor their work to the vision of literature set by male-dominated presses.

A central role was played by women readers who were hungry for feminist literature and supported it in the way that was most strongly felt under capitalism – by buying books. I remember coming out of an event during the first Feminist Book Week and being told by a woman in the audience that she'd spent her whole life reading books by men and now all she wanted to read was women's literature – books that were more about her.

The movement, which many writers were a part of, gave us a very special opportunity to develop. In turn our work influenced other women. We hoped to express the everyday experiences and needs of our readers and they were a support to us against the powers we threatened. Of course, it wasn't actually that simple. There were, on the one hand, many antagonisms between feminists and, on the other, support from small, left-wing, predominantly male presses, as well as some sympathetic editors and large presses jumping onto the bandwagon of a movement which could sell books. So, as has often happened in the past, a culture was developed out of a political movement for change. And recently, as that movement has taken on new forms, the culture has diversified and gone more into the main stream, while still having a feminist point of view.

Zoë Fairbairns – an example

Zoë Fairbairns is an example of a novelist who was both a part of and helped to develop the feminist movement. Originally she was in the

Feminist Writers Group, with Michele Roberts, Michelene Wandor and Valerie Miner. They created *Tales I Tell My Mother*, an early second-wave feminist book of short stories. She then wrote *Stand We At Last*, a family saga about women. The idea came from a joint effort between her and Virago Press. They not only published the novel, but read early drafts and gave her insight into the story itself. In this process we see the early role of feminist presses. *Stand We At Last* was widely read and helped to develop a sense of women's history. Since then Fairbairns has written other novels such as *Benefits* which brought feminist political arguments into the text.

Oranges Are Not the Only Fruit

In 1985 the feminist Pandora Press published the first novel of the lesbian writer, Jenette Winterson. *Oranges Are Not the Only Fruit* went on to win the Whitbread Prize and massive popularity. To top it off the BBC did a highly praised TV adaptation. This novel with its positive representation of a lesbian heroine came into mainstream focus because of the existence of Feminist Presses and the atmosphere created by the Women's Movement and the Lesbian and Gay Rights Movements. Winterson's involvement with Pandora Press was also as an editor of other novels including my own. Although other lesbian books have not been treated in the same way and there is still clearly discrimination, *Oranges* and its televised version by a woman producer and director does represent a milestone which was born of a woman's determination to define her own identity.

Feminist mysteries

Feminist authors have changed a number of literary genres, to use them from a woman's point of view. Doris Lessing has done this with science fiction and Angela Carter has used the fairy tale from a different angle in novels like *The Company of Wolves*. In the feminist mystery we see the questioning of the very limits of detective fiction which has so often stereotyped men and women in violent ways.

In Britain novelists like Gillian Slovo, Rebecca O'Rourke and myself have shown how this predominately male genre can be transformed to look at crime and **deviance** (i.e. being outside of what society considers normal) from a feminist viewpoint. We have done this by making the woman into the powerful figure of the detective then looking at truth and justice through her eyes. Right and wrong are redefined from an outsider's view, rather than trying to solve the mystery to reinforce and bring order to the present power structure.

Feminist mysteries question the very basis of that structure examining issues of gender and class. The female detective has a fuller personality with deeper feelings. As a woman she is concerned with the private world of family and friends (including personal relationships) as well as the public world in which the traditional mystery is solved. This affects the way she goes about solving the mystery and what it is she's really looking for.

In *Jumping the Cracks*, Rebecca O'Rourke looks at economic and sexual oppression and how they interrelate. By using a lesbian detective she creates a character who is outside the traditional view of power, moving beyond the boundaries of traditional social order. Yet it is this lesbian detective who brings order by solving the mystery. She also comes to a greater self-awareness about what it means to be a lesbian.

In *Death by Analysis*, Gillian Slovo shows the value of being concerned for others above selfish individualism. Her female detective uses dreams and feelings as part of her means of unravelling the mystery. As a socialist feminist Slovo sees the mystery as a way of talking about social issues.

In my mystery, *Vanishing Act*, the heroine must re-examine her relationship to movements for social change and her role as a woman in order to solve the mystery.

Black women writers

Black women writers have made an important contribution to second-wave feminist literature. Black British women and those who have come from Asia, Africa and the Caribbean have written about the joint effects of racism, sexism and colonialism, protesting against their treatment in Britain. Intermixing non-European languages and images in their work, they bring a rich diversity to British literature. As Lauretta Ngcobo points out in *Let it be Told*, Black women in Britain write to develop new models, breaking old stereotypes and creating a new sense of fortitude. The strength of their oral tradition has brought many Black women, like Grace Nichols, to use poetry (especially in performance) to reach a wider audience in the community. In *I Is A Long Memoried Woman*, Nichols describes the feelings and experiences of women in slavery, tracing their history.

I heard both Grace Nichols and the novelist Buchi Emecheta at a women's writing conference and found them each inspiring.

Emecheta, who put herself through college while raising her children and then building a writing career, has created novels which look at women's lives both in Africa and Britain. The semi-autobiographical *Second-Class Citizen* tells the story of a Nigerian mother who comes to Britain to face not only racism and poverty from society but oppression as a woman from her husband and the culture as a whole. In *The Joys of Motherhood* she focuses her powerful sense of observation on the oppression of women in Africa, breaking the taboo which pretends that they are content and secure.

Black women novelists have taken different approaches to the issue of being seen as a double outsider, both because of their race and gender. In *The Unbelonging*, Joan Riley symbolically examines the experience of Black women in Britain who are made to feel that they don't belong, even if they're born in Britain, while no longer belonging in the countries of their origins after so many years away. But in Barbara Burford's novella, *The Threshing Floor*, the presence of Black people is taken for granted as an accomplished fact. In the same way there is no sense of characters needing to justify or seek acceptance for their lesbianism. Freed of the conflict over belonging, characters are seen to make a positive choice when they enter into a lesbian relationship.

Asian women writers

As the Asian Women Writer's Workshop explains in the introduction to *Right of Way*, their book of prose and poetry, Ravinder Randhawa organised the first Asian women writers' workshop in Britain in 1984. At that point there were only a few Asian women who'd had their work published in Britain. Asian women came together not only to support each other and build their own confidence as writers, but also to gain more power and respect as a group. They wanted to have an influence on the publishing industry as well as on their own community.

When the group became more established, they had to deal with the question of how to define themselves. Some women wanted to call themselves 'Black', in a political sense, because they believed they faced the same kind of oppression as Afro-Caribbean women and that they needed to fight together. Others felt squeezed out of Black women's writing groups which mostly had Afro-Caribbean women in them. Some members felt that the cultural differences between Asian and Afro-Caribbean women meant that they couldn't respond to each other's work with the kind of knowledge which would have been helpful. To encourage young writers to join their workshop the group felt that it would be useful to have their name reflect the composition of the group. But they also decided to work closely with Black women's groups and take part in events for Black women writers. Clearly, there are many aspects to the issues of difference and identity for women writers.

The workshop helped members develop their writing and their confidence. They had group readings and discussions of their work. Putting together their collection or **anthology** took their focus away from building women's skills in the community. But it helped members of the group develop careers as writers. Some went on to become published novelists.

Feminist presses played a role in bringing the writing of Asian women to the public. The Women's Press not only published their anthology, but also the novels of some of the members of the Asian Women Writer's Workshop.

Both *Amritvela* by Leena Dhingra and *A Wicked Old Woman* by Ravinder Randhawa are novels which look at the experiences of Asian women who are between two cultures. In *Amritvela* the heroine returns to the home of her family in India after many years in Britain. And in *A Wicked Old Woman* the heroine, who lives in the Asian community in Britain, tries to make a life for herself beyond her traditional role.

EXERCISE 4.4

What are your opinions on feminist literature?

1 Have you read any of the books discussed above? If so, what was your favourite and why? If not, would you like to do so now?
2 Which kind of recent feminist literature interests you most? Why?
3 Have you read feminist literature from places other than England? (See the listing below for some suggestions.)

Feminist novelists from other places

As discussed at the beginning of this chapter, because of limited space I have focused on women who have written in England. Clearly, there are many feminist novelists throughout the world, whom I have not been able to discuss. On the next page are some suggestions of feminist novelists and their work, which you may want to read.

SCOTLAND
Ellen Galsford – *Fires of Bride*
IRELAND
Edna O'Brien – *The Girl With Green Eyes*
WALES
Catherine Merriman – *States Of Desire*
UNITED STATES
Maya Angelou – *I Know Why The Caged Bird Sings*
Valerie Miner – *All Good Women*
Toni Morrison – *Beloved*
Amy Tan – *The Joy Luck Club*
Marge Piercy – *Braided Lives*
Barbara Wilson – *Trouble In Transylvania*
CANADA
Margaret Atwood – *A Hand Maiden's Tale*
Joan Barfoot – *Gaining Ground*
AUSTRALIA
Patricia Grace – *The Sky People*
Katharine Susannah Prichard – *Winged Seeds*
NEW ZEALAND
Janet Frame – *Faces In The Water*
Rosie Scott – *Glory Days*
GHANA
Ama Ata Aidoo – *Our Sister Killjoy*
Flora Nwapa – *Efuru*
SENEGAL
Mariama Ba – *So Long A Letter*
SOUTH AFRICA
Besse Head – *A Question Of Power*
INDIA
Anjana Appachana – *Incantations And Other Stories*
Anita Desai – *Clear Light Of Day*
Shashi Deshpande – *That Long Silence*
Githa Hariharan – *The Thousand Faces Of The Night*
CHILE
Isabel Allende – *The House Of The Spirits*
INTERNAL ESSAYS ON WOMEN'S FICTION
Susheila Nasta (editor) – *Motherlands – Black Women's Writing From Africa, The Caribbean And South Asia*

Autobiographies and creative writing

Feminist literature is about women writing and that includes you. We all have our stories to tell and putting them down on paper helps to give us power. Often women start by telling their own personal stories.

Autobiography

Autobiographies have been used by many recent feminists to look at and analyse their own lives and the position of women in general. In the US, Rosario Morales has argued that women of color can best look at their cultural differences and understand their relationship to history through autobiographies. In Britain, Jean McCrindle and Sheila Rowbotham collected the life stories of working-class women in *Dutiful Daughters*. Well-known feminist novelists have talked about their histories and their ideas in books like *Fathers*. And Carolyn Steedman told about herself and her mother, who was a working-class single parent, comparing their experiences with how some male 'experts' stereotype working-class women in *Landscape for a Good Woman*.

Writing fiction

Many authors have found that it's best to start close to home with what they know and what's inside of them. If you begin by writing about your own life, you may find that the time will come when the story seems better if you changed things round a bit. If that happens, don't worry. That's the jump into fiction. You needn't feel as if you're lying. Often we've been brought up to believe that we have to tell the truth. But fiction isn't about factual truth, it's about emotional truth. Personally, I've found emotional truth deeper and more powerful. As I've built stories in my mind the characters have come together. Then, in a way, they come to life on the page.

EXERCISE 4.5 **Why not try writing?**

1 Write about your own history. Pick an event or point in time that interests you and just start writing. Don't worry if you can't remember every detail perfectly. (If you like you can add them in later or perhaps they're not really that important.) Just let yourself go. Let it come out. Don't think of showing it to anyone and don't worry about the spelling or punctuation.

2 Try keeping a journal just for yourself. Use it to think things out as well as telling what's happened to you. (I often use my journal as a way of getting the thoughts that are worrying me out of my head. Sometimes it helps me to understand them.)

3 Use something that's happened to you or that you've seen as a jumping-off point to write a short bit of fiction. Try not to judge it. Just let it come out. Enjoy seeing where your imagination takes you.

4 Take one of the pieces you've written from the ideas above and rework it. Don't be too harsh. Give yourself the freedom to write in whatever style suits you. Just try to get your piece to express what you want to say in a clear, understandable way.

5 Try to find someone you trust to read your work. Impress upon them that you're looking for support and constructive criticism only. Perhaps you can form a small writing group with this person and a few others. Whatever happens, try to enjoy the process.

5

MEDIA IMAGES, THE FEMALE BODY AND SEXUALITY

Beyond the images which try to contain us we are ourselves. What beauty in the diversity of our bodies. What energy in the power which abounds within us. What pleasure in our rich sensuality as we, ourselves, come to control our bodies.

Our body is our home – where we want to feel safe, and relaxed. A place we can call our own. A home we can enjoy.

Representations of women

Female images in advertising

Sexual objects

When we see a magazine advertisement with a woman in a tight, brief costume posing on top of a sports car or look in a tabloid newspaper and find a bare-breasted woman, we may well question the way these women are being used. Their bodies are being put on display to sell cars and newspapers to men. In these ads women have been set up as sexual objects. When this happens women are no longer being viewed as serious human beings but as things to stimulate men sexually so they will want to buy or do something.

Whose point of view?

Clearly, the two females I've just mentioned are being seen from the view point of a man. Too often advertisements show women from a male point of view. This means advertisers look at women through men's eyes using them as pawns in their own game of selling products and making profits. As well as using women's bodies as sexual objects, advertisers may also try to have their products thought of as female to try and make them seem 'sexy' and saleable. A famous example of this was a Fiat billboard which showed a picture of their car under the words, 'If it were a lady, it would get its bottom pinched.' As part of an on-going feminist campaign against sexist ads a woman added, 'If this lady was a car she'd run you down.' In this example we see the difference between seeing the ad from the male point of view of the advertiser and the female view of a woman who'd had enough of sexist adverts.

Women as consumers

There are many advertisements which are directed toward women as consumers, but even in some of these like perfume, make-up and hair colouring ads we find women making themselves over to please and attract men rather than themselves. Such ads can make women feel they need to buy these products to be beautiful, even if they can't afford them. But by creating a market for their product the company will make a profit.

Representations of women in the mainstream media

The **media** is various forms of mass communications like television, magazines, films, newspapers, etc. It has a very powerful influence on how women are seen and how we see ourselves. I will be focusing on the mainstream media, rather than the alternative media, such as small magazines which women may publish themselves. Certainly small publishing and video work plays an important role in telling about the realities of our lives and in giving us some control. But we also need to understand how we are represented in the mainstream media.

The servile housewife

Media images of women can not only reinforce sexist stereotypes about our bodies, but also about who we are. For example, we often see women cooking and cleaning as housewives in a way which is **servile** (in the sense that they are not independent but only there to serve their families). Such images keep up society's gender expectations that women should be responsible for the housework. They maintain the idea that whatever else women may or may not do what really counts is that they cheerfully service their family. It is not that our work as housewives and mothers is not valuable, to the contrary, women are not given credit (including financial payments) for the important work they do as housewives and mothers. But the media can put values on these roles for its own purposes. For example, images of 'successful housewives' are used by advertisers to manipulate women into thinking that they need to buy their products.

The role of media images

Media images can play a strong role in defining what is valuable in our relationship with others and within ourselves. Often these images do not reflect the reality of our lives, but construct an idealised image of femininity. These media images are used by others to judge us and we may find ourselves internalising them as a standard to judge ourselves as 'beautiful' or 'successful'.

Idealised images of femininity

The media's idealised image of femininity creates a mythical woman's body which is young, 'stylish', slim, free of body hair, odourless and white. As Kath Davies, Julienne Dickey and Teresa Stratford point out in *Out of Focus*, the majority of women cannot possibly achieve this idealised image of femininity because they are not young, white, able-bodied, heterosexual and wealthy. Women who don't achieve this ideal, or don't even what to, are viewed as 'strange'. The reverse of this is also true – images which reflect the reality of women's lives are rarely shown in the media. Instead we get the media's image of what we should be, which is something that we often are not.

EXERCISE 5.1

Look at various ads to see which kind of images of women you find.

1 Are they often being portrayed as sexual objects or as servile housewives?
2 How else are they being portrayed?
3 Do you find many images of women which do not meet the idealised image of femininity?
4 Pick out an ad which you feel is sexist and explain why you see it that way.

The role of the media

The media generally reflects the dominant values and expectations of society. It has a complex relationship with society as the media also influences society's values. Davies, Dickey and Stratford argue that the media tends to show capitalist, male-dominated society in a good light – to make it look like it's the best system. To do this the media needs to convince those who are less privileged that the basic problems and limits in their lives cannot be changed. If people believe this then heavy social controls aren't necessary because they will control their own behaviour. However, Davies, Dickey and Stratford believe that occasionally progressive information and images can come out of the media. There are exceptions and attempts to control information are not always successful.

The power of the media is in its ability to create and control images and information. In Chapter 2 we saw examples of how history books have silenced women's history and presented biased, partially correct or incorrect information. Media control of information and images has played an important role in keeping women apart, through competition. Women have sometimes been disempowered by internalising messages about themselves from the media. It has also helped to keep women from seeing the real power they could have by acting together, overcoming divisions like class and race.

Understanding how the media works can help women find ways to affect it. Clearly, it is a very complex institution, but it is still possible to make changes in the media's images of women.

Changing media images

During the last 25 years feminists have campaigned against sexism in the media. This has brought some improvements. There are now more images of women wage-earners and females being active, doing things such as sport. But when these images are examined closely too often it is found that the women in them still need to be glamorous and beautiful. In other words, the women are still on display. Of course, men can be on display. But there are a wider range of male images including those which show them in powerful roles. One way to decide how a woman is being used in an ad, for example, is to think about what the image of her would be like if a man was placed there instead.

Campaigns against sexism in the media continue. In 1994 women in the Writers' Guild of Great Britain and the Broadcasting, Entertainment, Cinematography and Theatre Union proposed a resolution on women's representation in the media. This was passed by the Trades Union Congress Women's Conference in Britain. It called for an end to women's invisibility in the news, more women in key decision-making and editorial positions, a greater reflection of women's diversity, more women contributors to programmes and the print media across all subjects and improvement in the range of women's images in the media. Clearly, a good number of women working in the media recognise the problems.

Some women in the media have suggested that in Britain women can have an impact on BBC radio and television if they ring up or write to the duty officer to complain about sexism in a programme they have seen or heard or to compliment it on its portrayal of women. They point out that each complaint or positive comment is logged in and distributed to those involved. Especially if there are a number of compliments or complaints about a programme this can have an impact.

Looking at different female media images

EXERCISE 5.2

Look at advertising aimed at children.

1 How are girls portrayed?
2 How is this different than the ways boys are portrayed?
3 How do you think this will affect the girls?

Girls

As Exercise 5.2 demonstrates, girls are generally portrayed in a different way to boys in the media. There are lots of examples of this from the images we find on birthday cards to those in comic books. As the Women's Monitoring Network points out, in comics boys are mostly shown as rough and aggressive while girls are presented as 'scaredy cats' and 'goody-goodies'. Women are almost always shown in family roles and Black families and children tend not to be shown at all. There are also far more male characters than females in comics.

In computer games almost all the active characters are male and too often the only female is the victim/princess waiting helplessly to be rescued at the end of the game. Both boys and girls are strongly affected by the media images they see and girls can be influenced by these idealised images of femininity, even if they contradict the positive realities of women around them.

EXERCISE 5.3

Look for images of Black, older, working-class, lesbian and/or disabled women in any form of media.

1 How are these women portrayed?
2 How often do you find them?
3 Describe one such image.
4 Are the women often in powerful roles?

Women and difference in media images

As discussed in Chapter 1, although there are oppressive expectations placed on all women, those women who differ from the dominant culture in society have additional oppressive expectations placed on them based on their age, race, ethnicity, class, level of ability and sexual identity. These expectations are expressed through images of women in the media.

Older women

Women get less and less media coverage as they get older. Elderly women are shown less often than middle-aged women, who are represented far less than younger women. On the whole, single, older women are represented the least. Youth is part of the idealised image of femininity, which is an important factor in the growing invisibility, by the media, of women as they age.

Because expectations of older women are that they are unhealthy and not interested in sex or fun, advertisers don't generally use them to sell products unless they are part of a specific campaign in which they are stereotyped. Too often older women are shown as victims of crime, as 'grannies' or as witches.

Although middle-aged women are often wage-earners, younger women who meet the idealised image of femininity are usually used as models even when selling products to middle-aged women. The reality of the strong, capable middle-aged woman is too often hidden or replaced by the stereotype of the ageing, complaining housewife.

As the Older Feminists' Network points out, aside from a few famous women, middle-aged and older women only seem to be deemed newsworthy when they play roles in the family such as wife, mother, widow or mother-in-law. Women who have been advantaged economically and/or educationally tend to get more positive media coverage than those on low incomes.

The wisdom and fulfilment of older women is almost always hidden by the media. Although recently there have been some improvements, too often the stereotypes remain or the reality of older women's lives are kept invisible.

Race

One way in which some of the news media has helped to maintain the unfair values of our society is by using Black people as **scapegoats** that is, putting blame on them which actually belongs elsewhere. For example, in Britain, Black people have been scapegoated as 'invading' immigrants and refugees who are 'job competitors', rather than focusing on the economic problems within the country. Too often Black men have been portrayed as threatening when crime, drugs and rioting are reported; while Black women have been presented as victims (of violence and famine) in need of protection by white society. In fact, the reverse is true.

As *Heart of the Race* points out, it is white societies which colonised and enslaved Black women in the name of civilisation. To justify their savage actions not only did Black people need to be seen as inferior but an image of Black women needed to be created which saw them as sexually promiscuous. This image lives on in the media in the form of the 'exotic Black seductress', like the night-club singer or prostitute. The other areas where we see Black women are in entertainment or sport.

For Black women to succeed in almost any role they must take on white cultural values including a white style of dress and speech. European values of beauty and culture have been exported all over the world. Not only do Black women find themselves outside of the white idealised image of femininity in appearance, but historically many Black women have had to develop characteristics of courage, physical endurance and self-reliance which threaten the media's image of women. Although there have been some improvements and we see more Black women on television than we used to, few are in decision-making positions.

Class

Since the campaign against sexism in the media started in the 1970s, there have been some moves to include the image of women as wage-earners. But generally if these women are given positive roles (beyond being sexual objects) they are shown as middle-class. Common Thread, a collective of working-class women writers, points out that especially on television, working-class women are either stereotyped as cleaners, cooks, prostitutes, housewives or victims. In any case they are usually seen as losers; with Black women, lesbians, women with disabilities and/or working-class women either being excluded or being set up in token roles.

It is middle-class life which is generally portrayed as 'normal', leaving working-class women in the bind of either seeing themselves in a negative stereotype or aspiring to lose their identity as being working class. Common Thread wants working-class women to define their own vision of themselves; and they want middle-class women to look at the role they play in perpetuating the class divide.

Jo Spence points out that images of working-class women as secretaries are different in advertising depending on whether the intended audience is a female or male one. For working-class women the secretary can be seen as one of the few positive jobs to aspire to. Advertisers often use this image with female audiences not to show the secretary actually working, but as a consumer at work. However, in magazines for predominantly male managers (not for her eyes) the secretary is seen as a tool, a source for company profit as a worker, rather than as a consumer. Traditionally, secretaries are viewed from a male perspective as a sexual plaything. So the secretary, herself, does not see images of her job as a valuable worker, although her employers recognise her value. This has contributed to secretaries not having a sense of their own power as workers who might take collective action with others.

Physical disability

Because the media creates its own idealised images of what is 'normal' and 'beautiful', they set an unrealistic standard which makes women with disabilities seem neither desirable or 'normal'. Negative images of women with disabilities not only affect the way they see themselves but how society sees and treats them. Images in the media help to create fear and give out wrong information about people with disabilities. Those of us who are temporarily able-bodied (during our lifetimes our abilities will change) need to re-examine our own images of people with disabilities and understand that society has built a disabling environment which creates greater barriers for them than their own disabilities.

As Micheline Mason points out, women with disabilities are usually left out of the media. When they are shown it is not as real people but as stereotypes. Pitiful little girls in wheelchairs are either embittered or able to walk if they just try hard enough. Too often women with disabilities are shown as helpless victims needing the aid of the able-bodied (especially men) to save them.

Because the state does not take the financial needs of women with disabilities seriously, seeing them instead as a burden, charities often use the helpless victim image to raise funds. Another stereotype exaggerates and romanticises the 'bravery and cheerfulness' of women with disabilities. This shows the low expectations of them by able-bodied society. Mason points out that women with disabilities need to represent themselves in the media and have editorial power over programmes and articles about them to truly change these stereotypes. To do this the information in the media must be made accessible to them.

Lesbians

The media's image of normality assumes heterosexuality is the only 'normal' way to be. Generally lesbians are ignored or they're shown as 'abnormal'. As Caroline Sheldon points out, they tend to be stereotyped as not 'really' being a lesbian but a confused victim of 'real' lesbians; as a 'butch' lesbian with short hair who dresses and acts in a way considered unfeminine (often being working class); as an older, wealthy, controlling lesbian or as an emotionally upset woman who often looks 'feminine' or is a closet lesbian.

As Julienne Dickey explains, the press tends to link lesbians with gay men and the AIDS epidemic, although lesbians have a very low risk of AIDS and the disease affects large numbers of heterosexuals. The tabloid and right-wing press especially play up and sensationalise negative stories about homosexuals, using them as scapegoats and whipping up homophobia, or they use them as a source of jokes and mockery. Lesbians are also used by some news media to discredit other groups such as the Left (to prove they're 'loony' for giving council money to projects involving lesbians); the peace movement (especially strong women's actions like Greenham Common) and feminism in general (to try to keep women from becoming involved with feminism and to try to create a division between heterosexual and lesbian women).

When television and films do show lesbians, too often they are tragic figures: sad, bitter, unattractive and/or unfulfilled. This does not reflect the diversity of lesbian women, who can be happy and fulfilled in successful, long-term relationships. The alternative press, the lesbian and gay movements and the feminist movement have helped to create a sense of pride and accomplishment, while recently lesbian writers and film makers have begun to show their own vision of reality.

EXERCISE 5.4

Look for images in the media which reflect the reality of women's lives.

1 Do you find images of all different kinds of women which show each of them as equally beautiful and important?
2 How often do you find images of women being thoughtful, strong and powerful?
3 Are women portrayed in a positive light when they are demanding their rights?
4 What images of women would you like to see in the media?
5 Try making your own images. Describe, write a script about, draw, photograph or put together images of women which you feel represent them fairly.

Pornography

Looking at how women are portrayed in the media brings us to the issue of pornography, about which feminists have strong, differing views. Although there isn't even an agreed definition, **pornography** can be defined as images or words which describe sexual behaviour that is degrading or abusive to children or adults, especially females, in a way that endorses their negative position. This can be different than **erotica** which can be defined as words or images about non-degrading, mutually pleasurable sexual behaviour between people who have the power to be there by choice. Gloria Steinem points out that pornography is about power and using sex as a weapon, while erotica is about sexuality. (I'll be defining and discussing sexuality later in this chapter.) But some feminists feel that it's not so easy to judge the difference between pornography and erotica, while others (including some lesbians) want to create feminist erotica.

Although most feminists have a gut reaction against pornography there are disagreements about what pornography stands for and what should be done about it. Some feminists see pornography as an extension of the sexist values against women which we have just looked at in advertising and the media in general. They want to work against pornography as part of a campaign to change negative images of women in the media, rather than focusing on it as a single issue. Feminists like Lynn Segal do not see pornography as being a direct cause of sexual violence against women although it does create a climate which condones rape. **Censorship** (i.e. the official inspection of media material, such as films and books, in order to forbid distribution if the material is considered objectionable) is not seen as useful for a number of reasons. These include a belief that censorship does not deal with the root causes of sexism (which include not only male domination but economics and racism) and because in a capitalist, male-dominated society censorship laws can be used against women and the movements for justice in which they are involved. Others oppose censorship because they want freedom of speech.

Feminists like Andrea Dworkin see pornography as the theory and rape as the practice. She believes pornography is the ideology which is at the source of women's oppression, defining what women are and how they should be treated; images of violence toward women and the hateful values behind them are made to seem normal and neutral. The reason for pornography is seen as male power; and the way of achieving that power is by degrading women. This view leads to seeing pornography as directly causing violence against women and thus wanting to outlaw it through censorship or stop it through direct action. The *Encyclopaedia of Feminism* points out that Andrea

Dworkin and Catharine MacKinnon wrote a model anti-pornography law, in the United States, which was later opposed by the Feminist Anti-Censorship Task Force.

— The female body and sexuality —

Women's bodies – subject or object?

When women look at adverts which show them from a male point of view, they may find themselves looking at the women as outsiders would see them. Instead of identifying with the woman in the image, they may find themselves identifying with the male point of view. Of course, there is more than just the male/female division in points of view. Sometimes women identify with a character because they are from their class or race or because they are handicapped or as old as they are. But what I am saying, as far as women's bodies go, is that too often the media presents women from the point of view of the male looker (seeing her as the object), rather than as the female who is inside her body (the subject). This means that we may get so used to seeing women from the outside as objects, that we can come to look at ourselves from the outside rather than feel ourselves from the inside as the subject of our own bodies.

How women relate to their bodies

Being the subject inside her own body means a woman tries to meet her own needs for pleasure, as she has a sense of what those needs are. She defines herself from the inside and has a feeling of being a whole person.

Being the object outside herself means a woman mainly thinks of her body as existing for the pleasure of others. Although she probably cares about how other women see her, she is doing this mainly for men. She may sees herself as a collection of body parts on display.

I have made a very sharp distinction here between a woman seeing herself as a subject or object. Of course, there are lots of variations between these two poles where many women fit in. But understanding the subject/object distinction can help us define our own viewpoint and needs which in turn can enable us to take greater control of our own bodies.

Too often we've been made to feel that we're the last person who should have any say over our body. We may have a sense that our bodies should be dictated to by style, the men in our lives and/or our doctors. Looking at society's image of our bodies and the relationship between our bodies and power can be helpful in understanding where our feelings came from. That can be a step toward developing more positivity toward ourselves.

Growing up female

The way we feel about our bodies has been shaped by our experiences growing up both within our families and in the outside world. Clearly, different families and cultures will have given us a different view of ourselves. But the values of our overall male-dominated society have had an affect on all of us.

As girls, society's female gender roles (see Chapter 1) helped to mould our view of and feelings about our bodies. We were more likely to be given baby dolls and fashion dress-up dolls to play with. This developed expectations that we would be mothers (whatever we knew or didn't know about where babies came from, clearly women's bodies were involved) and that fashion and how we looked was important to our identities. Fashion dress-up dolls set a physical body model. They clearly implied that we should be as slim and 'shapely' as our dress-up dolls, no matter what our body type or physical disability. With few exceptions dolls were white and blond-haired defining beauty in that way.

As the book *Our Bodies Ourselves* points out, society's expectations of feminine emotions affected the way we saw our bodies and how our sexual desires developed as we grew up. Women and girls were supposed to be more gentle, nurturing and concerned with emotions and the feelings of others, while men and boys were seen to be more aggressive. This, linked with the fact that generally we could see men had more power in the larger world around us, may have led us to feel that men should be the sexual leaders while we should follow.

As our bodies developed we generally learned that getting our periods was something which we must hide from men. Even if our mothers or other women did try to put a positive light on our beginning to menstruate, the process which gives us the power to reproduce our species is usually seen as a curse – something associated with pain, a strange smell and the fear of leaking through to our clothing, causing horrible embarrassment. Long ago when women were more powerful and highly valued (see Chapter 2 – 'The hidden history of mother goddesses') menstruation was seen as a mysterious moon-gift from the Mother Goddess. Imagine what different associations this set up about getting your period. Women could feel more powerful in their own bodies and could see their natural rhythm and body processes in a positive way. This would also have affected their sexual desires and fantasies.

As our breasts developed and our body took on a woman's shape our excitement and wonder at our own uniqueness was too often overshadowed by having to try to meet society's expectation of beauty. This often forced us to compete with each other and the images of women we saw in the media. All of us are different and each of our bodies can be pleasurable and wonderful in their own way. For example, large women can be seen to have more to love.

Recognising that a single 'standard of beauty' has kept women apart and often kept us feeling as if we're lacking may help us develop more positive feelings about our body. It is important to remember that it's taken a long time to develop any negative feelings we may have about our bodies and we need to be supportive and patient with ourselves if we want to turn that process around.

Suffering for beauty

As a girl I was told that I had to suffer for beauty. When I was growing up, curly hair was in fashion. My mother bought a home perm to 'beautify' my straight hair. I remember sitting there squirming as she dabbed this awful, smelly liquid onto the curlers she'd patiently rolled in my hair. It was when I complained that she told me about suffering for beauty. She had suffered, too, as the money to buy the home perm probably came from something she'd skimped on for herself. But that was the fate of women – to sacrifice, make themselves beautiful to get a man and then try to manipulate him subtly.

Can you remember what you were told about your body and being beautiful when you were growing up?

EXERCISE 5.5

As a way of examining your relationship to your body, circle your answer after each question or write your own answer.

1 Do you wear clothing which is uncomfortable because it's in style?
   ALWAYS   VERY OFTEN   SOMETIMES   OCCASIONALLY   NEVER

2 Do you know what you find pleasurable or only what you 'should' enjoy?
   YES   MOSTLY   SLIGHTLY   NO

3 Do we feel obliged to have sex or not to?
   ALWAYS   VERY OFTEN   SOMETIMES   OCCASIONALLY   NEVER

4 Do you question what is being done to you by the health system?
   ALWAYS   VERY OFTEN   SOMETIMES   OCCASIONALLY   NEVER

5 Do you take it for granted that doctor knows best and perhaps even knows more about how you're feeling than you do?
   ALWAYS   VERY OFTEN   SOMETIMES   OCCASIONALLY   NEVER

6 Do you have a sense that your body is something outside of your control which things are done to?
   ALWAYS   VERY OFTEN   SOMETIMES   OCCASIONALLY   NEVER

7 Do you get the feeling that your body is more like an image outside yourself which you and other people judge?
   ALWAYS   VERY OFTEN   SOMETIMES   OCCASIONALLY   NEVER

8 How do you feel about another woman's body when it is outside the standard view of beauty?
   POSITIVE   NEGATIVE   NEGATIVE, BUT THEN TRY TO CATCH MYSELF

9 Do you dislike parts of your body?
   ALWAYS   VERY OFTEN   SOMETIMES   OCCASIONALLY   NEVER

10 Do you try to remake parts of your body because you don't think of them as beautiful?
   ALWAYS   VERY OFTEN   SOMETIMES   OCCASIONALLY   NEVER

11 How much of the time do you feel that you live in your body from the inside rather than viewing your body in the mirror as an outsider would see it?
   ALWAYS   VERY OFTEN   SOMETIMES   OCCASIONALLY   NEVER

10 Do you try to remake parts of your body because you don't think of them as beautiful?
   ALWAYS   VERY OFTEN   SOMETIMES   OCCASIONALLY   NEVER

11 How much of the time do you feel that you live in your body from the inside rather than viewing your body in the mirror as an outsider would see it?
   ALWAYS   VERY OFTEN   SOMETIMES   OCCASIONALLY   NEVER

What do we mean by sexuality?

The word 'sexuality' gets thrown around when we start talking about our bodies and physical relationships. But what does it actually mean? Not everyone agrees and its meaning has even been changing. The idea of sexuality can be used in a broad sense or a narrow one. But many feminists see **sexuality** as the feelings and actions which come from desire. **Desire** is a feeling that you want or need something. In other words, I'm using sexuality in a narrow sense to mean how desire comes about (is created) and then how it's expressed.

The complexities of desire

Why is it that we find it pleasurable to be touched by one person but not another? Even if both people touch us in exactly the same spot we can have very different reactions. So what we find physically pleasurable is linked up to how we feel – to our desires. But how did we come to create these desires and how do they relate to our fantasies? As Lynn Segal points out fantasies often do not show us what we want in reality.

The reason – desire split

Jean Grimshaw believes that contradictions within women cannot be explained simply by talking about cause and effect. She discusses the split between reason and desire, using the example of women who have sexual fantasies which they would not find erotic in real life. She criticises the 'Images of Women' approach (uncovering oppressive images of women and then suggesting ways to replace them with positive images) because she says it fails to recognise and understand the appeal of these 'oppressive images' and the relationship they may have to a woman's fantasies, desires and concept of herself. She feels the 'Images of Women' approach fails to see that a woman might agree in her head that certain images were oppressive while still being committed to them emotionally or through her desires. Grimshaw believes all women (particularly feminists) have this split between reason and desire at some time.

Clearly, sexuality is a very complicated and complex thing. What's behind it? Where do our desires actually come from?

Where does sexuality come from?

The biological explanation

The Open University's *Study Guide for Issues in Women's Studies* points out that many doctors and scientists would argue that sexuality comes from our need to reproduce. They would say that our sexuality is a biological drive to keep the human species going – that sexual intercourse between men and women is meant to be pleasurable so there'll be children for future generations. This traditional view of sexuality focuses on the idea that it is a basic, natural, internal drive: this is an **essentialist** approach. Historically, the assumption behind this idea was that women were meant to be sexually passive and that there was something wrong with homosexuality. But if sexuality in people is just biological, why is it so different in different cultures? Why do some people not want to have children? Why do others enjoy having same-sex partners? And why do some people not want to have sex?

The psychological explanation

Psychologists would say that although biology is involved with sexuality, a lot of it has to do with the physical and emotional experiences we've had while we were growing up. They believe unconscious, unmet needs come out later in our sexual desires.

Seeing sexuality as socially constructed

Many feminists, like Carole S. Vance, have argued that sexuality is socially constructed. **Social constructionists** believe that sexuality is the product of people in society and history, therefore it can and does change. Sexuality is influenced by culture. They believe it may be thought of, experienced and acted upon differently depending on our class, ethnicity, age, physical ability, sexual identity and religion.

Social constructionists believe that sexuality is influenced by power relationships in society. Religious institutions and the state use their power to set out what is appropriate sexually. Power relationships are reflected in laws about sexuality. For example, historically women in Britain had to fight for legal rights in marriage and divorce. Today lesbian mothers have, at times, lost custody of their children. They also cannot legally marry their women partners. Clause 28 of Britain's

1988 Local Government Act prohibits promoting homosexuality by teaching or publishing material.

The complexity of sexuality

Society may play a major role in our sexuality, but what about our bodies? What about these very physical realities of our sexual experiences? Don't our bodies and society influence each other? The social constructionist, Carole S. Vance, questions these body issues but doesn't want this to take us back, full circle, to biological essentialism. Other feminists have felt that some biological factors could play a part without needing to see the role of biology as making women passive.

Sexologists (sex scientists) have played a role, as many feminists have been influenced by the importance of the clitoris in women's sexual response and orgasms. But although reports by those such as Masters and Johnson see sex as a healthy, enjoyable thing, it is still viewed as a biological drive. For many feminists focusing on the clitoris and women's sexual pleasure moves away from **phallocentric sexuality** (that is defining sex as being all about the phallus/penis and penetration). Phallocentric sexuality gives primary importance to male pleasure.

Lynne Segal points out that simply stimulating the clitoris is not enough – understanding the complexities of women's desires, including sexual fantasies, is essential. Although sex is problematic, she doesn't believe this is either because men are naturally aggressive sexually or because women have been cut off from their own natural sexuality. She rejects the idea of sex as simply a biological force seeing it instead as a problematic social issue in which ideas about sex need to change so that sex is not used to keep society's gender expectations in place.

Traditional heterosexism and lesbian existence

In male-dominated society a lot of fear has been built up around women leaving the heterosexual role. The traditional value behind this, which has been called **heterosexism**, defines homosexuality as 'abnormal' and also sees men as powerful and women as passive in heterosexual relationships. Many feminists see this kind of traditionalist heterosexism as keeping women oppressed. It is also linked to **homophobia**, the fear of homosexuality in other people and in ourselves.

Adrienne Rich looks at the issue of how choices about our sexuality have been socially constructed in her article, 'Compulsory hetero-sexuality and lesbian existence'. She argues that women are not given a choice about whether to be heterosexual or lesbian. The power of traditional heterosexism uses everything from physical violence to making lesbian culture and history invisible to keep the male right of physical, economic and emotional access to women. She uses the term **'lesbian existence'** in a broad sense not so much to talk about a physical act or desire but a broader emotional bond between women against male oppression and toward woman-identified experiences.

Sexual violence and rape

Most feminists agree that physical knowledge about sex must be understood in relationship to how it affects women within history and culture. But there are differing opinions about where this leads. Some feminists see the history and culture of phallocentric sexuality as leading to sexual violence against women. As the book *Women's Studies – a Reader* points out these feminists believe that when male sexuality is dominant, women are objectified and there is a belief that men have the right to sex with some women; rape and other forms of sexual assault will be a regular occurrence. Using male sexuality to keep women down will also be a weapon in colonialism and racism.

Catharine MacKinnon believes that sexual objectification of women through rape, violence and pornography is at the heart of women's oppression; sexual violence or the threat of it is used as a form of terror to dominate women. But her theories have been criticised for not giving credit to women's resistance and seeing them as victims. Also her strong focus on physical power has been seen as being at the expense of economic and/or social issues.

Other feminists believe women can have pleasurable sexual relationships with men in which they are not subordinate. Although sexuality is complex, they feel women's history and culture can be used to develop positive images of women which will enhance heterosexual and/or homosexual relationships. They see working against sexual violence as important, but view it in what they consider to be a larger context.

Male violence against women affects all of us and is an important issue for feminists. Although such violence includes rape, battering, child sexual abuse and sexual harassment, I will be focusing on the issue of rape here, as other forms of violence will be discussed in Chapters 6, 7 and 8.

Redefining rape

In *Against Our Will,* Susan Brownmiller showed how rape had been present throughout history and was seen not as a crime against a woman but against her husband or father, because she was viewed as his property. Second-wave feminists strongly disagreed with this traditional definition of rape as a sexual crime which is involved with property rights. Instead they redefined rape as a social institution which is used to maintain male dominance. In this definition rape is a violent crime against women which is all about power. No longer is rape seen to be about some men's sexual urges which can't be controlled or about women who, by expressing their sexuality, are 'asking for it'. Women demanded control over their bodies and an end to blaming the victim.

In *Intimate Intrusions*, Elizabeth A. Stanko argues that because women don't know when threatening behaviour will escalate into male violence, they feel vulnerable, must be on guard and develop avoidance strategies. Women who are young, poor and/or from ethnic minorities have a greater chance of male violence because, as a whole, they have less access to the resources of avoidance like cars. Part of these avoidance strategies involve women being seen as 'respectable'. The criminal justice system takes a male point of view on women's 'respectability' when judging and often minimising the effect of male violence on women, for example in rape trials.

Exposing the extent of rape – working against it

Feminists, especially radical feminists, exposed how common and widespread rape really was. They showed there was a far greater amount of rape than was reported. It was often difficult to report rape because women felt traumatised and ashamed. Although rape is a horrible experience, women did not feel that it was given credibility or that they were supported either by the police, the courts or the society. In the 1970s this led to the creation of Rape Crisis Centres for women-centred support. There were (and still are) campaigns to change laws, court procedures, police operations and society's male-dominated values about rape. There has been some headway made, but there are still many more changes necessary. Reclaim the Night Demonstrations have been held to empower women and point out the need to address the issue of their vulnerability, especially at night. Here is a poem I wrote in the mid 1980s about just such a march.

REPORT ON THE MARCH

'Women unite. Reclaim the night,'
we shouted through Cambridge darkness.
We took to the streets
with torches and placards
protesting the lurking of rape.
Men looked bewildered,
some jeered and some laughed.
But women seemed touched by our gesture.
They too felt our anger,
when after pub closing,
they'd also been stalked in the night.

Through Lion Yard we sang
of our spirit like a mountain,
voices echoing into corners
where women had been grabbed.
Empowered I shouted
my defiance held silent,
suppressed all those evening
I'd cycled madly home
evading the looming shadows.

We trooped back to the Common.
'However we dress, where ever we go,
Yes means Yes and No means No!'
we chanted at the drunks
standing about shouting, 'Whore!'
We marched through their phalanx,
stronger than threats,
and ended in a circle of song.

Men crashed through our ring.
Women enclosed them,
ululating our contempt.
Then we regrouped,
leaving in strength,
not letting ourselves be scattered.
But as we parted
I heard a woman ask,
'Is anyone going my way?'
'Yes!' Together
we'll make a time
when women can walk without fear.

Differing views about rape

As *A Feminist Dictionary* points out, feminists have different views of what the issue of rape stands for and what it means in the long run for women. Radical feminists like Andrea Dworkin see rape as the core of sexism. For her female oppression is based around women being victimised sexually and the culture defines rape as representing sexuality.

Socialist feminists see rape as part of a larger sexist system, involving other issues of gender as well as class and race. Simone de Beauvoir thought it absurd to link rape with all sexual intercourse. For her the issue was to create new sexual relationships that won't be oppressive.

Black feminists point out that Black women have not joined the anti-rape movement in large numbers because, especially in the United States, the myth of the Black male rapist has been used since slavery as an excuse to terrorise the Black community and because Black women rape victims have often been given so little support not only by the authorities but within the mainstream feminist movement. Angela Davis argues that Black women in the US have been organising against rape for over 80 years because they suffer such a great threat of sexual violence. Historically, there has been an assumption that white men, especially those who hold economic power, have a right to Black women's bodies.

Positive images of ourselves

I've taken the subjects of sexuality, rape and our bodies apart to look at the pieces. In examining these pieces we've seen many of the things which are wrong with the way society has constructed our sexuality. It was important to do this to have a clearer understanding of the forces which affect us and to acknowledge the pain we've suffered. I see the next step as putting the pieces back together in a positive way, using the knowledge and perspective we've gained to help us feel more in control of our sexuality and our bodies – to help us enjoy ourselves. Try the positive visualisation below as a first step.

EXERCISE 5.6 **Positive visualisations**

1 Sit or lie down in a comfortable place, where you won't be disturbed for at least ten minutes.

2 Let yourself begin to relax. Close your eyes. Take slow, deep breaths, releasing any tension with the out breath. Try to focus on your breath, letting go a little more with each out breath. Relax each area of your body in turn, starting with your feet and working your way up through your head. Think of a warm, soft feeling moving up through your body. Let the tension just evaporate out through your skin with your out breath.

3 Imagine yourself in a peaceful, enchanted place. It can look like some place you've been or be completely made up. Surround yourself with what you find most beautiful. You can be in the countryside on a summer's day with flowers, trees and warm sunlight or perhaps a quiet beach at the seaside. Take a moment to look around at the beauty surrounding you. Enjoy the colours and shapes. Savour the pleasure. Touch something there and try to feel the texture, perhaps the smoothness of a flower petal or the graininess of warm sand. Can you smell the perfume in the air or the fresh sea breeze? Perhaps you can hear some birds singing or the waves coming up along the shore.

Take a few minutes to get to know your special place then lie down there on a cushiony duvet. Now just allow yourself to become a part of the beauty which surrounds you. Let the harmony come in through your feet and slowly work its way up through your whole body. Perhaps you can imagine it as a warm glow, slowly enriching you.

EXERCISE 5.6 (continued)

Once you feel a part of your special place slowly get up from the duvet, keeping its comfort within you. Now imagine a lovely, reflecting pool of water near by. Walk to it. Look down into the reflecting pool and see the true beauty in yourself. Smile at your image, letting nature's harmony shine within you. Look closely at your reflection, note what you find most attractive. Now tell yourself that you're beautiful.

Turning away from the pool you notice other women happily coming toward you. They smile reassuringly as they approach. You don't know them but see that they're ordinary women. Each one is beautiful in her own way. Each woman is different. They can see the beauty in you, just as you see it in them. As they come closer you join hands around the reflecting pool. Encircling it, you look into the pool and discover the wonder of being together. It strengthens your own beauty. You laugh and the others join you. Of course, it's that simple. We are all beautiful. The reflection of each of us enhances the others.

4 When you're ready to leave your special place, do so slowly. Take a moment to return to thinking about your body. Feel yourself back in your body in the room that you're sitting or lying in. Starting with your feet allow a feeling of awakening to work its way through your body. Stretch and then open your eyes.

5 You can return to your special place as often as you like, either to repeat this exercise, to use it as a form of relaxation or to explore other issues by creating your own positive visualisations.

Redefining beauty

Remember the old saying, 'Beauty is in the eyes of the beholder'? This seems a good way of summing up the idea that beauty has been socially constructed and can be changed. In fact, what is considered beautiful varies in different societies and has changed over time. What I suggested in the visualisation is that there can be many forms of beauty for women. Rather than competing with each other, we can enhance one another. We can define beauty not as an exclusive value but as an inclusive one.

Clearly it's not easy to wake up one morning and have a different vision of beauty. There's all the pressure from the media and society, our upbringing and often a sense of shame which we feel about our own body and what has happened to it. But a first step in changing the way we view beauty can be to start by looking at ourselves.

Improving body image

In the book *Bodylove*, Rita Freedman points out that **body image**, the way you picture your body, is connected more closely with the way you feel about yourselves than the way you actually look. By focusing more on enjoying your body you become the subject of it, rather than an object. She suggests techniques to improve body image. These include self-praise and **affirmations** – saying good things about yourself over and over again, which can help to commit you to positive change and a healthier way of seeing and thinking about yourself. My mother used to say, 'It's all the way you look at things.' Remember we can change the way we look at ourselves. Catching those automatic negative thoughts, refuting them and creating positive ones can be helpful.

EXERCISE 5.7 **Self-praise and affirmations**

1 Think of the physical things about yourself which you find attractive. Write down some true compliments about your body and the general way you look.
2 After coming up with a list of what you like about your body, look it over to see if it conforms to the stereotyped image of femininity. Perhaps a second, creative look at yourself will help you move beyond focusing on the praise you've heard from others to a deeper appreciation of yourself. Here are some examples of this:
   My round body has a womanly fullness.
   There is a sense of confidence about the way I hold myself.
   My dark eyes send a powerful message.
You can refer back to your praise list to help challenge negative thoughts.
3 Use a mirror. Look yourself in the eye and voice one of your praises. Use the same praise over and over again for a few days.
4 Repeat a more general affirmation which could be about accepting yourself. For example I've been saying, 'I accept my grey hairs as a sign of wisdom.'

Sensuality

Developing **sensuality** – pleasure through touch, taste, smell, hearing and seeing – can also be important. This involves focusing on your senses and savouring the enjoyment you can get from them. To do this you may also need to look at the sense of shame about your body which you may have internalised from society's views.

Increasing sensuality can develop sexuality, but it needn't be seen as leading to a sexual goal. There can be so much pleasure in just getting to know your body and becoming more intimate with yourself. Your body, which is your home, can be a cherished friend.

EXERCISE 5.8 Self-touch – rediscover and explore your home

1 Lie comfortably. Close your eyes and relax, following the instructions in part 2 of EXERCISE 5.6 (positive visualisations).
2 Use your fingertips and the palms of your hands to touch, massage and pet your face and hair. Feel the different textures and sensations.
3 Work your way downward, exploring other parts of your body. Take your time. Allow yourself to feel and enjoy the various sensations in your hands and in your body.
4 If you wish, you can move to the more sexual experience of focusing your touch on your clitoris. Many women find this pleasurable.

Finding beauty in our changing body

Over the years and through accidents and illness our body and level of ability changes. We are not stagnant like the idealised image of femininity. We are vibrant and alive – changing and transforming. We can find beauty in that process and the challenges that it brings. Through those challenges we gain knowledge and learn about ourselves. This helps us to understand and respect the changes that others go through.

Our body image needs to change with our body. This means accepting the loss of our old body image and developing a positive view of our new one. Our body changes can be a slow process, as with ageing, or more dramatic, as in the case of accidents or sudden illness. Either way we can come to our own terms with these changes, rather than accepting society's vision of what we have become. We can make room in our definition of beauty for more diversity.

EXERCISE 5.9 **Choosing our own models**
(rather than letting the media do it for us)

1 Think about, research and ask others about admirable women whom you can identify with in some way. Try to choose women who have become the subject of themselves rather than glamorous objects. Such women might be writers, scientists or wise and/or heroic women (whether they are famous or living down the road). See how many such women, alive or dead, you can find. What qualities about them are attractive to you?

2 Choose one of these women. Observe her or find pictures and information about her. What has she achieved of value? How does she seem to feel about her looks? Study her body to see how her success is expressed through it. Having found positivity in her body, locate it in your own. It is not a question of copying her, but of using her example to create your own style and appreciation of yourself.

3 Use her image as a counterbalance to the idealised image of femininity you see in the media. Be on the lookout for more models. Choose new ones as your body changes. Create new affirmations.

6

WOMEN'S HEALTH, WOMEN'S MINDS

Oh the pleasure and delight in our own well-being – the freedom to relax, feel good and be ourselves. Such wondrous potential unlocked as we come to harness our own physical and mental powers.

Women's health

EXERCISE 6.1

As a way of thinking about the whole idea of health, try answering the questions below.

1 What does it mean to you to be well or ill? How would you define these words?
2 Try to imagine a healthy person. What do they look like?
3 What factors have made you ill in the past? Do they include economic, social or cultural influences?

Who decides what is 'illness' or 'health'?

This question of who decides what is 'illness' or 'health' may, at first, seem foolish since these are terms we take for granted. But like history or standards of 'great literature' when we look more closely we find a value judgement behind them. Natural female processes like childbirth are classed as health problems. Discomfort during menstruation or the menopause is seen as illness. Often these processes are referred to as 'women trouble'. Medical statistics and society's view of women generally sees our visits to the doctor about our reproductive processes, including those for contraceptives, as being about health problems. This implies that our bodies themselves, our very ability to give birth (if we choose), is a health problem. The less non-problematic, truly healthy body is generally seen as male. It is this male vision of health which sets the assumptions of what is 'normal'. This affects how we look at and feel about our bodies.

The shape of health

It's as if the idea of health has been created as a narrow, rigid box and we keep finding ourselves trying to squeeze into it. Why does health have to take that form? Why can't it be a loose, round shape into which women can move around during the many cycles of our lives? If the idea of health was more flexible not only could it take in a larger number of women, allowing them to feel more comfortable about their bodies and their inner sense of well-being, but it could also include groups of women and men such as those who are disabled. For just as the idealised image of femininity is a stereotype which excludes most women, a rigid expectation of 'normal' health is basically a view of well-being which is seen to belong to white, wealthy (or middle-class) men.

Health reflects power

Health reflects power not only in western industrial society but in the developing world. Those groups of people with less power, including women, are generally excluded from the vision of 'normal' health. And they tend to have less access to what is seen as the best health care. These factors affect their well-being. People with less power generally suffer from social and/or economic influences which prevent them from reaching their health potential. In other words, lack of money and/or social status can be obstacles to well-being, which affect many women.

In the developing world we can see how health is reflective of the power of the West. The economic power of the West means that instead of having fairer relationships with the developing world, which would raise standards of living and promote health, the West dictates policies like population control. Although birth control can be very useful to women when they choose it, population controls are often imposed on women, taking away their power to make decisions about their own bodies and their lives. At the same time, far higher infant mortality rates and **maternal deaths** (women dying either in childbirth or from unsafe abortions) show the lack of economic resources and political power held by women in the developing world.

Medicine and money

Medicine is big business, even in countries like Britain with a mainly free National Health Service (NHS). In recent years government changes have created an 'internal market' in the NHS as well as a growing business in private health care. In the US it is not unusual to hear of ill and injured people being turned away from private hospitals because they cannot show that they will be able to pay the bill.

Both the medical technology and the drugs industries are based on profit. To make profits they need to be sure there will be a high demand for their products, whether or not that's in the best interests of the women involved. Of course, drugs and medical technology have been useful to women, though perhaps not as much so as their makers would like us to believe.

Feminists have questioned issues such as the extent of the use of drugs and medical technology on women, who makes decisions about their use and what's in the best interests of the women involved. In the end this gets back to the issue of control of women's bodies and the basic question of whether medicine should be based around profit or need.

Medicalisation

Medicalisation is defining people as 'ill' or 'healthy' and then using this view in dealing with people who are 'ill' and the whole idea of 'illness'. Catherine Kohler Riessman sees medicalisation as happening on three levels. Conceptually medical knowledge is built up using scientific method which limits both the kinds of problems studied and the kinds of models used, oversimplifying processes into cause and effect. Institutionally this happens in the way hospital treatment is organised and interpersonally in the way doctors treat patients, using scientific method (whether or not it's appropriate) to bolster their authority.

Medicalisation takes different forms. For example, Riessman discusses the oppressiveness of the medicalisation of obesity i.e. seeing it as an illness. Ann Oakley has written about the medicalisation of motherhood.

Male-dominated medical science

Medicalisation and health standards were created by a male-dominated medical profession and the male-controlled institution of science behind it. As I write this what comes to mind is my wonderful woman doctor. In fact, the National Health Service in Britain employs large numbers of women, but very few of them are in positions of real power, especially involving overall policy-making decisions. Most women are nurses or in lower-rung positions where they are not able to challenge the male vision of medicine and health. Of course, women in and out of the health system have brought about some changes in the last 20 years and there are some sympathetic male doctors, but that doesn't change the fact that western industrialised medicine is based on a male point of view. This has created opposition to the women's health movement from organised medicine and other traditional groups in society, such as the political right wing.

Strategies for change

Feminists want to create a women-centred vision of well-being which questions and changes the quality and quantity of health services that women get. Sheryl Ruzek points out that although feminists want women to have more control over medicine, their bodies and their reproductive possibilities, there are different strategies for achieving this. Liberal feminists work to gain equal opportunities within the system, focusing on getting safe, efficient medical care for women. Radical feminists want to completely reorganise the system, questioning conventional medical treatment and the use of 'professionals' for much of women's routine care. They have worked to create alternative services run by and for women, which involve self-help. Socialist feminists want to raise awareness about how industrialised capitalism causes basic problems in women's health care. They work to extend and redefine state health benefits to include all women, trying to eliminate limitations based on class and race.

The differences in feminist strategies have caused debates. But there has also been unity, especially around specific issues like a woman's right to choose to have an abortion. And, of course, we must remember that not all feminists fall neatly into categories or work accordingly.

Types of projects

The women's health movement, growing out of the women's liberation movement, came to understand that difficulties which individual women were having were based on larger issues. Too often we ended up feeling like there was something wrong with us, individually, rather than questioning the expectations of women by society, examining the social impact of industrialised medicine and looking at the way in which health was socially constructed. In order to confront issues of power in health care, women needed to organise together and mobilise. They educated themselves and made information available to other women, created alternative services and worked to change public policies. Many different groups and projects have been formed. These range from well women clinics and women's health centres, which focus on women's needs and give them more control, to campaigning childbirth pressure groups like AIMS in the UK, which works to improve maternity services within the National Health Service so women can make informed decisions about their care and midwives can have a stronger role as practitioners. And from women's health material written from a feminist point of view, such as the pioneering book *Our Bodies Ourselves*, to reproductive rights campaigning organisations, which are particularly strong in the US where they've had to fight for basic rights like national health care and regaining a women's right to choose to have an abortion.

Reproduction and power

Issues of reproduction have been at the core of the women's health movement. For women to take control of their lives and plan their futures they must control their ability to bear children. Clearly, this ability to create another generation of life is a tremendous power. Biologically, being able to bear children (whether or not we decide to do so) differentiates us from men. So the big question becomes who controls our very special biological ability, which directly affects our health and our future?

Our power to reproduce has been seen as a threat to male-dominated society which had to be controlled. Over time, this has taken different forms including making sure that some women remained virgins until they were controlled during marriage. Other women, such as Black slaves, were used as breeders and even surgically experimented upon. More recently women in Nazi concentration camps were used for experimentation involving their reproductive capability.

Today there are a number of important issues involving the question of who controls our reproductive power. The idea of an **unviable foetus** (tissue which is developing into a new life but cannot as yet survive outside the mother) having rights which can even be seen as more important than the rights of a grown woman has been used to take away our control of our bodies. This concept of the 'right to life' has been utilised, especially in the US, as a weapon against women.

Many feminists would argue that in the West an over-reliance on technology and medical intervention has been used by male-dominated medicine to take control away from women during reproductive processes, such as in unproblematic childbirth. Poor and/or Black women in the West and women in developing countries have been pressured or tricked into **sterilisation** (being made to be unable to have children). In some parts of the world women have been forced to have abortions if they are carrying a female foetus. In the developing world women have been used as guinea pigs for experimentation of new birth control methods.

Women's reproductive rights

Since the start of the 1980s the term 'reproductive rights' has been used to bring together the many issues involving women and reproduction. **Reproductive rights** are the rights of women to choose if, when and how they want to have children. This involves the right to control our bodies and has been interpreted to take in a wide variety of issues. These include everything from a woman's right to choose to have an abortion, which women in the US have recently had to fight to retain and even regain in some states, to ending sterilisation abuse. And from birthing rights to the right to health care, child care and contraception.

When I was in the United States in the late 1980s, I was active in the Portland Reproductive Rights Committee. We did everything from organise demonstrations for the right to choose to have an abortion (as part of a larger national movement) to holding local workshops on various topics and from building alliances with women from different communities to working for national health care.

Gaining knowledge and power

In order to truly have reproductive rights we need to have the knowledge to make informed choices and the power to do so. The women's health movement has found that to gain these things women need to meet and campaign together. That very process not only gives us a chance to pool information about our bodies and the health system, but to understand more about how we see ourselves. Together we can build our own confidence, create alternative services and/or help each other as patients' advocates in the health service and effect policy decisions on women's health.

EXERCISE 6.2 **Your views on women's health**

1 How have your experiences of health and health care been influenced by being a woman?
2 What changes would you like to see in health services involving the treatment of women?
3 How are you influenced by your present stage in your reproductive life cycle?
4 What do you think about reproductive rights?

A personal note

Having hot flushes has been a part of the whole process of my writing this book. Sometimes it's meant I've been woken up in the night and then began to think about some point or other I've been researching or writing about. Other times I've been sitting at the word processor and suddenly needed to take off the jumper I was wearing over my blouse or even, occasionally, stop and lie down if the hot flushes included strong palpitations. Usually, I reflected on what I was writing or went back to reading for a few minutes.

Although the hot flushes have, at times, been disruptive they have also grounded me in my own body and my present experience. It's not as if I wouldn't mind them going away. But I also feel it's important to say that my hot flushes have been part of the process of discovery, reflection and writing that is this book.

A friend of mine just told me that hot flushes have been renamed power surges. I like that. I'll try thinking of them that way.

Women's minds

Balancing the outer picture and the inner view

When we start to think about our own mind or the mind of any individual woman, can we hope to understand it without looking at the wider picture going on around us? Each of us is unique with our own thoughts and problems. Yet we are all influenced by the society around us. Economic, social and political factors can't help but affect our state of mind. And women of different classes, races, ethnic backgrounds, levels of ability and sexual orientations will experience these factors differently. If a woman is a single mother living on income support with four children in a damp council flat how can this not influence the way she feels? The way we see things and feel about them does not just come from within our minds, it also comes from the outside world.

Our mind is affected by our own individual history, historical forces taking place around us and our position within society. Being a woman is a factor in all of those. **Psychology**, the study of the mind, needs to be seen within a broader context which includes gender issues.

On the other hand, it would be a mistake not to look at psychological aspects and just blame everything on society. For example, last year I taught an inspiring Black woman student who was raising four children on her own in inner London. After doing a Return to Learning Course, she completed an Access to Science Course and went on to University. Clearly state of mind is more than purely environment. The inner world and the outer world interact in complex ways.

Putting women in context

In *Women in Therapy and Counselling*, Moira Walker describes three ways to look at a woman to increase an understanding of her by putting her in context. These are knowing and accepting her as an individual, looking at her family history and being conscious of the influences of the society at large.

Influences on girls and women

To gain an understanding of our minds, it is important to see how girls are raised to view themselves. Even today when there is more promise of equality, girls receive different and often mixed messages. **Sex differentiation** (that is different attitudes and treatment of females and males) is linked to economic, social and political structures. As we have seen earlier, society's images and expectations of girls greatly affect how they see themselves.

Baby girls

The first messages baby girls get generally come from their parents, especially their mothers. Nancy Chodorow believes that mothering is a universal element of the sexual division of labour. She argues that a girl's identification with her mother means that she grows up with a **relational identity**, which is defined by her relationship with others. A man has a **positional identity**, which is defined by his position in the power structure of society.

Mothers affect how girls grow up to see themselves, although there are also other important influences. A study by Ann Oakley in 1979 showed that far more mothers were pleased to have given birth to boys than to girls. Daughters brought out more negative and less positive feelings in their mothers than sons did. Other evidence has shown that boys get more attention and stimulation than girl babies from their mothers, who are more concerned about the appearance of their daughters.

Perhaps in the 1990s attitudes of a new generation of women have changed, but I suspect overall the above is still generally true because new mothers have, themselves, been influenced by male-dominated society and the mothering they received. Even though many mothers do try to raise daughters in a different way, they often find the influences around them still affect their daughters.

Mothers and daughters – the double bind

In *The Reproduction of Mothering*, Nancy Chodorow talks about the **double identification process**, where mothers identify with their daughters and girls with their mothers, because they are the same sex and the mothers have been girls. She believes that mothers of baby girls do not tend to experience them as separate from themselves in the same way they do with baby boys. This strong identification, coupled with society's stereotypes, makes it harder for women to let their daughters develop independence.

From a girl's point of view she must be like her mother to develop and keep a female identity; at the same time to become her own person she must separate from her mother. This double bind causes conflicts for many mothers and daughters who may basically love each other. For daughters this may create difficulties in establishing an identity of their own and in dealing with conflicting expectations and demands. Mothers may recognise issues which are similar to those they went through with their own mothers, even when their lives are very different.

Education and jobs

Gender is only one of the factors affecting women and girls. We see this clearly when we look at education and jobs. Working-class girls are more likely to be seen as troublesome in school, to leave education early and end up in low-paying, low-status jobs. Working-class and immigrant girls are more likely to lack confidence in their own abilities. Black girls and those from ethnic minorities may find themselves stereotyped in negative ways which limit their education and job opportunities.

Although class and race play an important role, gender expectations affect girls overall. Studies have shown that troublesome boys in school get the most attention and that teachers spend more of their time with boys than girls.

Those of us who grew up in past eras will certainly remember how girls were counselled away from what was seen as 'men's jobs'. I remember when I started university in 1964, as the first member of my immediate family to do so, it was common to hear that girls only went on to university to get their 'Mrs'. I was annoyed by this, as I wanted to be taken seriously. But I also saw that (in those days) most women gave up their careers once they had children and I accepted that marriage was part of my future. My mother encouraged me to become a school teacher as this was a career a woman could return to after her children grew up.

Although there are less overt pressures on younger women, many of the old expectations remain as well as sexual harassment. It takes a lot of confidence and effort to enter a field like engineering, which is still a male preserve. Women often feel lonely and isolated studying subjects and fighting for jobs which are considered to be 'men's work'.

Girls and women may have mixed feelings about career success, as there's an underlying expectation in society of unpleasant futures for women who are clever and successful. This goes back to the idea of women not being too clever or successful so as not to threaten men. Also girls and women are often concerned about the issue of how to manage being a good mother and a successful worker. Considering the studies, published in 1995, showing improvements in girls' exam scores in Britain, it's amazing how much has been achieved under difficult conditions.

Relationships

From an early age much of a girl's life generally revolves around relationships with others. This seems to be even more so for working-class girls who have fewer models for a future profession. Boyfriends often feature strongly in teenage girls' thoughts and actions, whether or not they have one. Most girls still seem interested in marriage and having children in the long term, even if they want to do something else first.

Very few young women see their future life with no partner, although many women live happy, successful lives on their own. Though it may not be true, there is still an underlying expectation of security in male support. This goes beyond economic dependence, which has been used to hide the emotional dependence that men often feel for women. The myth of a need for male security involves the knowledge of male power that girls are generally raised with and the underlying social unacceptability of female independence. This combination of encouraging dependence and denying independence works against a woman's sense of her own power and creates conflicts between a desire for a life on one's own and having a family.

Women's emotional strength

In spite of, or perhaps because of, a female upbringing in male-dominated society women often have enormous emotional strength and perceptiveness. There is also an emotional richness and power that women often feel together. With all the problems we face it is important not to lose sight of the power and potential we hold in our own minds.

Implications

To understand the issues and problems that women face we must have some knowledge of the process of growing up. Moira Walker points out that our upbringing has meant that many women tend to descend quickly into guilt, blaming themselves, anxiety and low self-esteem. With an understanding of the effects of gender stereotyping it becomes clear that a woman's guilt, depression or anxiety does not come only from her own mind. By recognising the role played by the inner world and the outer world we can see the uniqueness of our own individual minds while coming to understand that we're not alone.

Motherhood and a woman's identity

Whether or not we want to, can or do have children, women are generally defined by society as mothers and care givers. This has a strong effect on our lives. Women who are not able to or don't want to have children can end up feeling that they are somehow going against what is supposed to be their mothering instincts. Even if a woman has resolved the issue within herself, if she is in a relationship with a man others may wonder about her not having children. This stems from the expectations of male-dominated society that a woman wants to be in a relationship with a man and that she wants children. If she is independent or in a lesbian relationship then society reacts differently. Although nowadays the stigma of single parenthood is far less powerful than it used to be, we still see many governments using single mothers as scapegoats when it's politically convenient for them. And lesbian mothers still fear having their children taken away.

[handwritten margin note: maternal expectations of society]

Psychological effects of motherhood

Whatever we decide to do with our lives, it is useful to understand motherhood, because it holds such a central position in society's view of a woman's identity.

Pregnancy

Pregnancy brings enormous changes to a woman's relationship with herself. Her physical self, her body, is something she is now sharing. If she does not decide to have an abortion and doesn't miscarry, she will give birth to what is growing inside her and it will be her own child. Whatever else this process is – wonderful, difficult or more likely some of both – it is dramatically different. She is no longer alone and her body is no longer completely her own.

In the later stages of pregnancy, as her physical and psychological boundaries change, a woman tends to gain more of a sense of a baby growing inside her. This also becomes clearer to the world around her, which affects her identity, as does her feelings about becoming a mother.

At birth there's the discovering of this new human being with its own personality, while there's still somehow a sense of attachment. If the pregnancy has been difficult giving birth can be a great relief, while for other women it can be experienced as a strong sense of loss. If childbirth goes well it can bring a precious, happy time, but it can also open up or reinforce a sense of confusion about a woman's own identity. Clearly this is a period when women are vulnerable. (See Chapter 7 for more details.)

Relating to medical professionals

Having a baby for the first time can be the occasion when a healthy woman begins to have prolonged contact with doctors and hospitals. Although some women are seen by family doctors or midwives and specialists who will deliver the baby, many end up in ante-natal hospital clinics. Some studies show that these women often feel uncomfortable about asking questions and do not have a chance to get to know the people who will be with them during the birth.

As discussed earlier, childbirth is not an illness and yet its medicalisation can leave women feeling both alienated from their own body processes and unable to get the information they need to help them feel less anxious and more in control. Being just another name, waiting in an unfamiliar hospital clinic, is an example of the contradiction between society's ideal of motherhood as a woman's highest goal and the reality of women finding themselves with low status during pregnancy and then as mothers.

Relating to a partner (if a woman has one)

If a woman has a partner there will generally be changes in their relationship during pregnancy and after the birth, especially with the first baby. Their lives will change dramatically from two free adults to people sharing their space and time with a demanding, new human being. For women this is also a time in which they often lose their economic independence. This raises issues of dependency.

Paid employment

When and if a woman does return to employment the chances are she will do so part-time. And full-time employed mothers still have a change in status. Employed mothers with a baby at home often feel they are struggling to meet the demands of being Supermum. Conflicting demands of work and motherhood play a pivotal role in the lives of many women.

Relationship with female friends and relatives

A mother's relationship with female friends and relatives also generally changes. She moves closer into the orbit of other mothers with children the same age as hers. These relationships are often supportive, although they can also be limiting. A new mother now has a shared experience with female relatives and especially her own mother. This can lead to conflicts as well as comfort.

Need for support from others

No matter how great it is to have a baby a woman is still caught up in a whirlwind, which leaves her tired, trying to balance various emotional needs. If she has a partner he or she may also feel this. Some partners are very involved with caring for babies (although others are not), but for mothers the intensity of changes of lifestyle and sense of self is greater. During this time a woman may well feel resentful or isolated if she doesn't get the support she needs.

The relationship with the growing child

The bond between a mother and her growing child can create powerful feelings in a woman. Some of these relate back to her own upbringing. As the child develops the mother generally goes through many more changes. Just as her lifestyle and sense of self altered after the birth, it continues to change as the child develops and there are new demands. This can leave a mother feeling as if she's doing a balancing act between her own sense of herself and her connection with her child or children.

EXERCISE 6.3 **Looking at mothers and daughters**

1 What kind of a relationship did you have with your mother? How was this affected by you both being female?
2 What do you think of Nancy Chodorow's idea of the relational identity of women? How has being a woman affected your relationship with others?
3 How has your identity been affected by society's expectations of motherhood?
4 In what ways do you see women raising their daughters differently nowadays? In what ways are they raising them as they had in the past?

Violence against women

Violence against women is not just an individual act. It often has society's approval, for example it is used in wartime or as a form of terrorism by dictators. In places like Bosnia we've seen how this includes rape, which was used as a tactic of domination against the 'enemy's women'. Historically, wives have been considered their husband's property, which gave them the 'right' to batter or rape them. Until the end of the nineteenth century men had a legal right to beat their wives in Britain. Violence, including sexual abuse, against children also has a long history as they were considered to be the possessions of their father.

It is almost always men who make war and have been seen to have the right to possess women and children. Violence is an important aspect of power in male-dominated society. And violence against women is far too common. According to Oxfam statistics one woman in every 2,000 has been reported as raped worldwide. But this figure does not give an accurate picture as large numbers of women don't report being raped. Studies in the US and UK consistently show that 75–90 per cent of rapes are not reported to the police. And in England and Wales the conviction rate for rape has fallen dramatically; according to official crime statistics the conviction rate for rape has fallen from 32 per cent of complaints in 1977 to 18 per cent in 1987 and only 10 per cent in 1993. Figures concerning domestic violence in England and Wales show that half of all homicides of women are killings by a partner or ex-partner and a third of all crimes against women result from domestic violence according to the Home Office. According to NCH Action For Children, a woman dies at the hands of her partner or ex-partner every three days, and only 2 per cent of domestic violence incidents are estimated to be reported to the police.

Psychological effects

Women who experience violence, or have in their childhood, often feel a sense of psychological distancing or alienation from others. Especially if the violence came from someone they thought they could trust, there can be a strong attack on their sense of themselves. Childhood abuse can eat away at the foundation of a person, making the process of rebuilding it difficult.

Violence against women cannot be psychologically explained away with the idea that women are somehow clinging to abuse because of earlier violence against them. This could lead to the myth that women enjoy abuse or are 'asking for it'. Although some women who were abused as children become caught up in a pattern of violence (from the home, to school, to their own adult partner) other women do not become involved in violent relationships as adults, although they may well feel the affects of their earlier violent experience. It is the violent behaviour, itself, which is better explained by looking at the violent partner's abusive childhood. A study by Martin and Kalmus showed that it is violent men who came from abusive families, rather than women survivors.

Childhood abuse

Although both boys and girls are sexually and physically abused, girls have a much greater chance of being sexually abused by their father or other men than boys do by women.

In looking at the feelings of women survivors it is important to keep in mind that they have not only experienced a lack of power because of individual male violence, but also from the more general misuse of power by male-dominated society.

Feelings of women survivors of childhood abuse
A woman survivor can feel like a little girl who has been very hurt and betrayed by someone they trusted. Although survivors were not able to control what happened to them, they may feel guilty and responsible. Placing the responsibility on the abuser and building trust with others can be a difficult, though achievable, process. There may be a huge sense of loss and a need to grieve. This process can lead to anger about the abuse which needs a safe place to be expressed. Survivors need to come to trust themselves and take control of their own lives.

Women and violent partners

Women are in a double bind when they find themselves in a relationship with a violent partner. Not only must they deal with the abuser but there are also societal factors involved like disadvantages in getting decent jobs and housing and lack of child care.

Difficulties in leaving a violent partner
Financial and other practical problems can be difficult for women

trying to leave violent partners, but there are also other factors. Because there are strong societal expectations that women should be in relationships and are somehow responsible for them, leaving even a violent relationship can make a woman feel like a failure.

Abuse can leave a woman feeling scared and powerless. Violence can bring on a feeling of numbness, as if one does not actually exist. Not only is it hard to act in this state, but women often fear men will come after them and hurt them even worse. But battering is potentially life-threatening and though it can produce a crisis of confidence many women do leave violent partners, often using refuges set up by feminists. Women can take back the power over themselves and build successful lives.

Survivors of rape

Rape is a crime of power. As such it can be terrifying and degrading. Rape is also used as a threat to limit women's activities and feelings about being able to move about freely, especially at night. Yet the reality is that many rapes are committed by men who are known to the woman and often happens in a woman's own house, which she had felt was safe. This kind of betrayal of trust can be extremely painful, confusing and overwhelming. There are far more cases of rape than are ever reported to the police.

Support for rape survivors – their feelings
Since the 1970s there have been Rape Crisis Lines and support organisations set up by feminists. There has also been a growing awareness of the need to support rape survivors.

Right after a rape a women is in an immediate crisis in which her requests should be taken seriously. These usually involve the possibility of calling the police, psychological support and medical help. With younger women there is also the issue of telling their parents. A woman may feel the need to retell the details of the rape repeatedly over a long period of time. It can be useful to be able to express anger. Women may feel that they were somehow to blame, even though this wasn't the case. They can feel that they have become bad or dirty. Some women have a delayed reaction.

Moira Walker argues that although rape will affect a woman's relationship with men, most women want to be able to have positive relationships with men in future. Therefore, she believes an anti-rape stance in counselling should not imply that all men are responsible. (See Chapter 5 for a detailed discussion on rape and this issue.)

EXERCISE 6.4
Looking at violence against women

1 What experience have you had with violence against women and how has this affected you?
2 How does this relate to the values of our society?
3 What should be done to end violence against women?

Effects on women's mental health

Depression

Large numbers of women suffer from depression. It is a painful and isolating condition which affects far more women than men. Although there are higher rates of depression among all ages of women, which are continuing to rise, young women are particularly affected. This is especially true of women at home with young children. Working-class women have been shown to be more likely to be depressed than middle-class women. And working outside the home seems to make women less likely to be depressed.

Why do women get depressed? – The hormonal myth
One theory about why more women get depressed is that there is a hormonal basis to women's depression. This is a very convenient way to shift responsibility away from male-dominated society and onto women's own biology. It can lead to seeing women as inferior and not 'normal', again defining 'normal' as being male. Gail Vines sees the use of hormonal explanations as a way of trying to pin down identity in a time when social identity is seen to be changing.

Although some women may be affected by their hormonal changes this narrow view not only stands in the way of building a caring approach to women, which looks at the whole person, but shifts the blame onto women themselves ignoring social conditioning. An example of this is the old myth that menopausal women necessarily get depressed. In fact, a study by Reid and Yen showed that there is no evidence of increased risk of depression at this time. The difficulties middle-aged women and those with young children face are far more involved with society's expectations and treatment of them.

Depression – what women say
Moira Walker gives a number of reasons why women themselves feel they get depressed. Because women often take on the responsibility for relationships, they may blame themselves when they break down. They may fall into the trap of having their identity secured by their relationships with others, especially a male partner, their children or their parents. Too often women's expectations for achievement, fulfilment and security in life don't match up to the realities of their opportunities, financial rewards, marriages and the conflicts, anxieties and low status of motherhood. This is especially true for Black women, women with disabilities and working-class women.

Depression – the trigger of loss
It has been suggested that some form of loss is often a trigger for depression. Women tend to have many losses and disappointments, though other factors such as class and race are also important to take into account here. Women may experience a sense of loss in childbirth itself or from giving up or losing part of their financial independence and work status, which often follows. The shrinking of their world and social contacts can feel like a form of loss. Battering, sexual abuse and harassment can create a sense of loss of part of one's self. Miscarriages, abortion and not being able to have children may also be experienced as loss. Children starting school or leaving home can be other forms of loss. There is also a sense of loss in women's lack of opportunities and general treatment as second-class citizens as well as past losses, especially the loss of a mother in childhood, which may play a role.

Buried anger
Society's expectations of femininity do not include, and actually help to suppress, a woman's expression of anger. This pent-up, repressed anger can turn into depression.

Working against depression – the protection of employment, college or outside interests
Lack of working outside the home has been identified as a factor contributing to depression for women. Employment has been seen as

a protector against depression for women partially because it gives them some financial status and independence. I would expand this to say that beyond employment, further education and other outside interests could also serve as a protective factor. It is that experience of being yourself out in the world again which is often so important to mothers with young children. Although it can be extremely exhausting, waged working or going to college is a way that a woman can maintain and develop an identity beyond motherhood, if she finds that helpful.

There are times when decent paid work is not available or employment is not a suitable option for women on benefit, who may lose more than they gain. In these cases further education or training may be helpful and may also help women get a better job later. This is especially important for working-class women whose high rates of depression may by partially attributed to their low status.

Working against depression – the barrier of lack of child care
I can just hear you saying, 'That's fine, but who'll mind the children?' Although sometimes women's training courses will provide child care, generally this is a real barrier. It is also a clear example of the contradiction between society's expectation for women (especially lately with a demand for women to take low-paid, part-time work) and the reality of women's lives which involves lack of child care facilities. But during the Second World War, when women were needed in the factories, child care was provided.

The devaluation of motherhood, and women in general, often leads to women's isolation and depression.

Working against powerlessness
I don't mean to suggest that there are quick, easy solutions to the pain of depression. But for some women a feeling of being powerless or being out of control is part of depression. Exploring ways to have more control over one's life may be helpful. Talking to a friend or going to a Women's Centre or self-help group may be the start of that process.

Working with a counsellor or therapist to untangle things can be useful. Therapy or counselling to overcome depression should keep in mind the social realities for women as well as their own internal dynamics and family histories.

EXERCISE 6.5 Looking at depression

1 How have you or other women you've known been affected by depression?
2 What relationship do you see between depression and society's expectations of femininity?

Eating disorders

In order to understand eating disorders, which are mostly experienced by women, it is useful to see them in the context of society's expectations of femininity. Traditionally, women are expected to prepare food in the home. They are often judged by how well they do this. So women spend a lot of time thinking of and actually buying, preparing and serving food. In this way women can come to feel that part of their value depends on food. And yet there is a massive contradiction for women because at the same time as they are supposed to be good cooks for others they must not eat too much themselves if they are to strive for the thin, idealised image of femininity. The underlying message seems to be – make for others what you can't have yourself.

In Chapter 5 we looked at the idealised image of femininity, which is so powerfully constructed by society, and how most women could never achieve this image (although not all women want to) no matter how hard they try. But it is that trying, that internal reflection of society's value of slimness for women involving an image of adolescence rather than maturity, that has played a role in eating disorders.

Eating disorders are complex and there is no quick, simple answer. But to begin to try and understand them it is useful to look at the context in which women find themselves.

Throughout the world there are many women and their children who are hungry. In this way food is literally power. But food can also have symbolic power. In a family where a daughter feels she can not exert her own power, not eating and becoming extremely thin may be seen as a kind of political act, almost like a hunger strike. As women are trying to gain power over their lives they may become obsessed with food and the desire to have absolute control over their intake of it.

Anorexia

Typically, **anorexia** involves extreme loss of weight coupled with an end to menstrual periods. The anorexic woman sees herself as overweight, while others are worried about her severe loss of weight. She can't recognise that she needs food and if this continues long enough it can lead to her death. But she is generally interested in food, which often comes out in behaviour based on obsessions with food. This includes being very interested in (and gaining pleasure from) making food for others, while not feeling able to eat it. Here we see a reflection of society's contradictory messages to women concerning food.

The wide-spread treatment for anorexia in many hospitals is to pressure a woman to eat until she reaches a certain weight, generally by not letting her get out of bed or dress until she does. Although this can achieve weight gain it does nothing to resolve the psychological issues which caused the anorexia in the first place. Susie Orbach argues that a traditional psychiatric approach can actually become part of a woman's problem because by denying the meaning of a woman's symptoms and not acknowledging her protest they help to perpetuate her symptoms. What can happen is that after such hospital treatment a woman can feel she has completely lost control. Because she doesn't want to repeat this experience she may become bulimic.

Bulimia

Bulimia is eating to excess and then vomiting afterwards. This process can be kept secret because a woman can generally keep to a weight which is considered to be normal. Many women with anorexia become bulimic or move between the two disorders, although not all women with bulimia have had anorexia.

Because of earlier hospitalisation women may be afraid to reveal their bulimia and may see it as a way of taking back some control. But with bulimia, food and the pattern of bingeing and vomiting can dominate a woman's life and make it hard to have close relationships for fear of discovery.

Alternative therapy

Feminist therapists like Moira Walker make it clear that a woman herself must have control of her eating. They see the use of food in eating disorders as a way of communicating and work with women to understand the complexities of the message behind this. Acknowledging that long-held patterns are difficult to give up, they try to take the fear out of food by looking at the subject in a relaxed manner, without setting target weights.

EXERCISE 6.6 Looking at women and food

1 How would you describe your relationship to food?
2 How is this affected by you being a woman?

Feminist counselling, psychiatry and medicine

Feminist counselling and therapy

Feminist counselling is a perspective, rather than a technique, which takes in practitioners from different theoretical backgrounds. It believes in building an equal relationship between client and counsellor, although this does not mean that they are the same. Feminist counselling brings a political stance into therapy, assuming that structural changes are needed in society. It believes a major cause of women's problems is the social reality and rejects the idea that women should just adjust to society's needs. It takes the approach of coming to understand both the inner and outer world as a way to not only empower women, but to help build self-confidence while finding choices and possibilities for the future.

Psychiatric and medical care

Historically, women have had little or no say over policy-making in psychiatry, although women have been the majority of patients. Psychiatry and medicine have both been male-dominated professions. Tranquillisers have been over-prescribed in 'treating' women, causing great distress. Being tranquil has been considered a desirable feminine quality, while being angry has not. Certain behaviour and symptoms were seen as more acceptable in men than women. In fact, some characteristics in women have been considered to show mental illness, while in men they're seen as mentally healthy.

During the anti-psychiatry movement of the 1960s R. D. Laing argued that women's symptoms, which were considered signs of madness, were actually a way of both trying to make sense of a situation which was senseless and a way of dealing with demands which were contradictory.

Recently there have been more separate counselling and therapy services for women outside psychiatric facilities as well as a greater awareness about not over-prescribing tranquillisers for women, who have been the main recipients of them. The feminist critique and the growth of feminist counselling have helped to develop an awareness of the importance of gender issues in therapy. We can also hope that as more women enter psychiatry and medicine there will be a greater sensitivity to society's expectations of femininity and the wide variety of women's actual behaviour.

Psychoanalytic theory and psychological research

Psychoanalytic theories

Although there have been disagreements among feminists about psychoanalytic theories, ideas growing out of the Lacan approach and object-relations theory have played an important role in feminist thought. (See Feminist Literary Analysis in Chapter 3 and Psycho-analytic Feminists in Chapter 1 for details.) This is because these psychoanalytic theories have been useful in understanding gender relations and the unconscious. They look at and try to explain **subjectivity** (the inner forces within a person's mind) taking into account their social position.

Those psychoanalytic theorists following the approach of Lacan have looked at Freudian ideas like 'penis envy' in a less biological, more symbolic way. They see the phallus (penis) as the signifier and language as the symbolic system which defines women as 'lacking maleness'. But Lacan has been criticised for reinforcing negative stereotypes of femininity and still seeing validity in the biological.

Psychoanalytic theorists following object-relation theory look at the human drive to form relationships. The most important time for them is the earliest years when a baby is focused on its relationship with the mother. (See Nancy Chodorow in the section 'Mothers and daughters – the double bind' in this chapter and Psychoanalytic Feminists in Chapter 1 for details.) But they have been criticised for putting so much importance on the mother-baby relationship that it reinforces traditional, male-dominated values of femininity.

Psychology

Until recently psychological research has mostly ignored gender differences or, like much else in science, viewed the masculine as 'normal'. Psychology has been interested in accounting for mental processes, looking at the mind like an object. Although women's experiences have been described, when looking for the causes of problems, gender issues have not been a focus until recently.

In the 1980s the academic area of Psychology of Women was recognised after a successful struggle to show the importance of social and political relationships. This has led to research which is based more on women's real lives. It has challenged the idea that 'femininity' is created individually rather than being socially constructed.

The relationship between psychology and psychoanalytic theory

As far as women go, both psychology and psychoanalytic theory have tried to find and explain the source of behaviour and experiences which characterise females in society. But they have gone about this in very different ways. Psychoanalysis is focused on subjectivity (what's going on from within), while mainstream psychology, especially research, sees the mind as more of an object to study from the outside.

Coming back to our strengths

After having looked at various issues in the area of women's physical and mental health and documented many of the ways women have been disadvantaged, it is important not to lose sight of the enormous power which so many women possess. Often this power goes unrecognised because what women do is undervalued by society. For example, there is the inner power it takes for a mother to get her children off to school in clean clothes with packed lunches when she has the flu or is depressed.

Let us examine our strengths. I have often been inspired by the emotional strength and physical endurance which so many women possess. Why not look at yourself and acknowledge your strengths? Too often women are so busy supporting other people that they find it difficult to credit themselves.

EXERCISE 6.7 **Crediting your own strengths**
(Now don't be shy and skip this one.)

1 In what ways have you used your inner strength and/or physical strength for your own well-being and the well-being of others?
2 Make a list of your positive qualities. How have they been helpful to yourself and others.
3 How could you be more positive and supportive toward yourself?

7

FAMILIES

Family – that warm sanctuary that drives you mad. Glowing hugs somehow fade in endless piles of dirty washing. Even sharing the drudgery doesn't change the way visitors look at the woman when the house is messy. And all the years of pretending not to care doesn't change the fact that part of you still does. Of course, it's more important to put your heart into the kids. But the value of all that energy used raising them won't pay for a bus ride into town. One hand busy at home, while the other's working outside. Keep juggling. Keep those balls moving through air. Watch the Balance. Balance, while trying to find space for yourself.

The personal is political

When the Women's Liberation Movement began to build in the late 1960s and early 1970s one of the strongest ideas that came out of us meeting together and talking was that the personal was political. Nowhere was this more true than when we looked at the home. What so many of us had thought of as our own personal problems with the men we lived with took on a new meaning when we began to see political patterns. We saw that if a woman argued with her man about him doing the washing up or changing nappies this was a political issue. Suddenly we were not alone in our own private battles. It actually mattered who cleaned the toilet and who had time to read the Sunday paper.

Politics wasn't just something out there. It was a very practical process in our own homes which could help to free us. By seeing the personal as political our demands were no longer petty nagging; we had a right to be taken seriously. Instead of saving up our complaints until they bust into tears, we could make rightful demands for men to do their share of the housework and child care. Although some relationships didn't last under these new arrangements, others profited from it. Many of us became involved in new relationships with a different vision of what they should be like. These new visions took a variety of forms including communes, single parent families and **non-traditional families** (where two people, who may or may not be married, have an equal partnership, sharing tasks such as housework and child care, if they have children).

Over the last 25 years there have been changes in family life and much talk about 'the family', but for me that starting point of the personal being political is still worth keeping in mind at home and in employment.

What is 'the family' and the family ideology?

Just as 'normal' physical and mental health have been defined as male (usually white, middle-class), the 'normal' family has been seen as a white, middle-class, breadwinning man and a dependent wife and children. The image of the **'cereal-packet' family** (a male breadwinner with his dependent housewife and children) is one that the majority of people don't fit into; just as the idealised image of femininity doesn't fit most women. In Britain in 1990, only 44 per cent of the population lived in families which consisted of married couples with their children and more than half of those that did had two breadwinners, according to the Central Statistical Office. If we look at it in terms of households, we find that only 28 per cent of British households were made up of a married couple with dependent children. The cereal-packet family is not the typical household unit, but keeping up society's image of it is a political act to maintain the family ideology. **'The family' ideology** is based on the mistaken idea that there is only one kind of family and that it is somehow 'right' and 'natural' that the man be the dominant breadwinner, the woman the dependent housewife and that they 'should' have children.

Just as the media's idealised image of femininity keeps many women feeling that they're somehow lacking, the cereal-packet family image is used to judge other kinds of families as lacking. This has been combined with racism in Britain to stereotype Afro-Caribbean women as single-parent matriarchs whose children are endlessly exposed to different men, while Asian mothers are viewed as failures because they're seen as passive victims who refuse to learn English and integrate into British society. But in reality families take many different forms.

History

Historically, families have changed over time and there is no 'natural' basis for men being the breadwinner. The myth that men have always been the breadwinner is untrue. In Western society, before industrialisation created factories with large machines, most production revolved around households. Men, women and children were involved in farming, crafts and/or household industries. They all contributed to the economic survival of their family, although men usually had control of the resources which were seen to include their wives' labour.

It was only with industrialisation that production was taken out of the household. This divided off domestic work done at home, which was unpaid, from waged labour. From this came the nineteenth century idea that women's 'natural' place was in the home and that there should be a 'family wage' earned by the male breadwinner in the outside world. (See Chapter 2 for details.)

Although by the twentieth century the 'normal' family in Western society was seen as being the male breadwinner and his wife at home, not everyone lived this way. For example, there were always working-class women who were (low-paid) wage labourers.

As the twentieth century draws to a close, most people are not living in the kind of family which our society would like us to believe is 'normal'. In Western industrial society there are many single-parent families and a large number of working mothers, as well as unemployed fathers. And in most non-industrial societies women either make a large contribution to or are the main providers of food.

The effects of culture on families

Various cultures define families differently. This includes basic issues such as who is classified as kin relations, the role of mothers and fathers, marriage arrangements and childrearing.

It is important to look beyond our own experiences and expectations to see that women of different ethnic groups have different experiences in families. This is true for women of various ethnic groups in Western industrial societies as well as for women in the developing world.

The effects of class and race

Middle-class, professional women often use their higher level of educational qualifications to develop wider roles in the outside world and seem to have greater freedom than working-class women. Black and/or working-class women (who, as a whole, are more likely to have lower status, less satisfying jobs) have argued that mothering, the caring part of domestic work and the creating of a home are positive, satisfying experiences. Women who are oppressed in the outside world based on their race or class have argued that family life can create needed support and a more positive identity. But dislike of repetitive housework is widespread.

The effects of sexual preference

The most basic thing about the cereal-packet family is that it's heterosexual. The setting of this 'norm' makes lesbian and gay families the 'other' just as single-parent families have been judged that way. This has led to lesbian mothers being viewed as 'deviant', thus questioning their ability to be 'good' mothers, although there are many successful lesbian mothers. This view has been used in child custody cases brought by ex-husbands, resulting in a number of lesbian mothers losing custody of their children. It is also used as a threat creating stress and fear for lesbian mothers.

Lesbians can be a part of many different family forms. But because of 'the family' ideology they cannot legally marry and often can not receive health or pension benefits from their partners.

Feminist views on families

Although feminists have criticised 'the family' this is not because they are against everything about family life. And their critique is not meant as an attack against women living in families. The purpose is to come to understand why and how the **traditional nuclear family** (a dominant, male breadwinner with a dependent housewife and children) within capitalist, male-dominated society has kept women down and what can be done to change the family roles which women find oppressive.

Looking at all kinds of families

Feminists look at women's roles in all kinds of families and how they have been affected by 'the family' ideology. For example, although nowadays a large number of mothers are employed, (even if they may take time off when the children are young and/or return to waged work on a part-time basis) most mothers who are employed do a double shift because they are still expected to be responsible for the housework and child care. Even when women in a nuclear family bring in a big part of the family income (or the biggest part) there is still somehow an underlying expectation by society that they are just working for family 'extras' with the man being the real breadwinner. The standard set by 'the family' allows society to judge single mothers as lacking, just as it does women who choose not to have children. It also presumes that no matter what arrangements a man and woman may make between themselves to share child care and housework, any slip-ups are the fault of the woman. Although the times and economic realities have changed, the legacy of 'the family' ideology lives on to haunt us. It is by coming to understand how and why this ideology has been used to oppress women that we can begin to truly move beyond it.

Seeing the positive side

Especially lately, examination of family life has been done with a recognition that families can also be a place where women gain meaning and self-worth in their lives. (Black feminist theory has played an important part in making this point.)

Viewing families in a wider context

In the 1970s 'the family' was seen by many feminists as the centre of women's oppression. Perhaps this was because as the Women's Liberation Movement began to develop, enormous discontent with family life was uncovered. In consciousness raising groups women expressed their anger both at the men they lived with and at the way they were undervalued as housewives and mothers by the world around them. Patterns of isolation and even violence began to come out of the family closet. The reaction to this was that something dramatic had to be done quickly. There were blazing issues around the family, so the fire seemed to be centred there. But now it is generally felt that women's roles in families should be looked at and understood in the wider social context of female oppression. This has affected some feminist points of view. For example, instead of just seeing women's domestic work as the reason why women are disadvantaged in the job market, there is now more of a sense that limitations on women's paid work are often a cause of female domesticity.

Main approaches

Most women are involved in some form of family relationships, which are important to them, and feminists see the need to understand women's roles in families in order to deal with their oppression. But various feminists have emphasised different aspects of family life in trying to understand and redress women's oppression. Male violence and control of women's sexuality and reproduction have been one focus. Another is the economics of unpaid domestic work and how that contributes to capitalism, or the way men benefit from women doing the housework and child care. Another approach is looking at how the state, religion and/or culture strongly affects family life. Examining the affects of difference in class, race, ethnicity and sexuality on families has been a recent topic of discussion.

What's behind 'the family' ideology?

Beyond these different approaches, and often underpinning arguments within them, is the basic question of whether 'the family' and its ideology works in the interest of patriarchy, capitalism or both. Understanding this can help us to see how families have ended up being as they are, what the vested interests are and what are the most effective ways to create change.

Differing feminist views

Radical feminists

Radical feminists have argued that it is men and patriarchy that benefit from 'the family' and its ideology because men hold an unequal financial power relationship with women and because patriarchy gives men the 'right' to dominate their wives, including using violence. Kate Millett described the family as a patriarchal unit inside patriarchal society which served as a stronger force to ensure conformity than others forces like religion.

Marxist feminists and socialist feminists

Marxist feminists have argued that 'the family' and its ideology works in the interest of capitalism because women produce labour power in the form of the next generation of workers (children) and care for the needs of the present generation. Social stability is also created and there is control of workers who don't want to take action that will hurt their family.

The difference between this Marxist view and a socialist feminist view is described by Jane Prince as being that although women of all classes can be sexually oppressed, Marxists see it in the financial interests of bourgeois women to keep economic exploitation going through the class system. Therefore, not all women are economically exploited, though they may experience sexual oppression. But because economic exploitation is seen as the main force behind oppression, the focus of struggle to end sexual oppression is linked to class issues.

Some feminists would argue that nowadays with the inclusion of issues of difference and more of a focus on the oppression of women in paid employment, the difference between Marxist and socialist feminists (which is considered a broader term) boils down to a question of emphasis.

In the 1980s Lynne Segal and others examined the family ideology and the future of family life more deeply in *What is to be Done About the Family?*

Discussions about housework's economic value under capitalism led to the 'domestic labour debate'.

Materialist feminists

Some feminists got to the point where they felt the domestic labour debate was leaving out the whole issue of men benefiting from the domestic labour of their wives.

Materialist feminists like Sylvia Walby put forward an alternative argument that men exploit the labour of women in the home within a patriarchal mode of production, which exists in relationship with the capitalist mode of production. In other words, individual men benefit from their wives doing the housework and reproducing and caring for children, if any. Although the men themselves are exploited as workers, housewives typically work longer hours but get less money for their own use than their husbands.

This argument can include women who are working outside the home and also doing the housework and child care. They not only tend to have less leisure time, but less money to specifically spend on themselves.

Black feminists

Black feminists have argued that family life can create needed support and a more positive identity against oppression based on race and class in the outside world. Writers like bell hooks have criticised white feminists for focusing on the family as a base of women's oppression. Black feminists have shown that colonialism, slavery and immigration laws affect Black families. For example, during slavery

Black families were specifically broken up. And in Britain today there are many examples of Black families being split up through government deportations.

Gemma Tang Nain points out that Black feminists do recognise that family-based oppression of women is possible, because there are specific expectations of women's roles in families which mirror those in the wider society. But she adds that even in white, middle-class nuclear families, which have been the focus of feminist criticism, there are positive things.

Liberal feminists
Liberal feminists, many of whom are in the United States, work for legal and social reforms to better the position of women in the home. But they do not call for radical changes either to capitalism or patriarchy. They want to create changes in laws and educate people around issues such as abortion rights, child care and maternity benefits. In the US women tend to have less rights in these areas than in Europe.

Overview
Clearly feminists, and women in general, have mixed feelings about families. Perhaps because women are so much a part of family life it is especially hard to sort this out and gain perspective. Although I have presented different feminist views about families, things aren't always this clear cut as it can be more a matter of emphasis. Women with differing views work together on many issues relating to families. And some feminists have argued that non-sexist families can be not only freeing for women, but emotionally freeing for men.

Various family forms

Single-parent families – a major family form

The single-parent family is a major family form and can neither be dismissed as 'deviant' or 'exceptional'. In Britain one in five families with dependent children is headed by a single parent according to the General Household Survey of 1991. Nine out of ten of these families are headed by single mothers. Over the last two decades the number of single-parent families have grown dramatically. Although many single mothers have been divorced or separated after living with a partner, since the late 1980s there's been an increase in the number of younger, single women who have decided to have children without living with a partner.

Single mothers deserve respect not economic hardship
Single mothers play an important role in society, raising the next generation which will build the future, and deserve recognition and respect not economic hardship. Although single mothers make a valuable contribution to society, single-parent families have a significantly lower standard of living. In Britain, according to Labour Research, in 1992 only 17 per cent of single parents work full time. Clearly lack of child care is a major issue. Around 70 per cent of single-parent families live in poverty or on the edge of it, while only 20 per cent of two- parent families do. The difference is dramatic in housing, as demonstrated in the General Household Survey. Less than 30 per cent of single parents own their own home, while over 70 per cent of couples do. Just about 60 per cent of single parents live in council housing, while only 20 per cent of two-parent families do.

Much of the difficulties which single mothers and their children face such as poverty, lack of good, extensive child care and decent housing are based on the notion that they are a threat to the 'normal' way of life and should not be encouraged. In other words, when you just look at things from the point of view of what maintains society's values based on profit and male domination, then single mothers are seen as lacking. But when the care of children is viewed as valuable, then single mothers are seen to make an important contribution. Children are no longer called 'legitimate' or 'illegitimate' depending on their relationship to their father. But single mothers are often still conveniently blamed for society's lack of concern for children, while child poverty is allowed to continue.

There are many successful single-parent families, even though single motherhood can be isolating and difficult in our society. Single mothers can be strong and independent. Although the economic situation has to be taken into account, some feminists have suggested that single mothers experience less stress than mothers who are unhappily married, as well as having more independence and a sense of satisfaction from being able to handle things by themselves. Single mothers also organise and take part in support networks. Among Afro-Caribbean single-parent families, who have the highest proportion of this type of family in Britain, single mothers are often part of a support network involving female kin and other local community members.

Non-traditional families

In a non-traditional family two people, (who may or may not be married) have a mutual partnership where tasks such as housework and child care, if children, are the equal responsibility of both partners. Clearly such a relationship goes against traditional expectations and is difficult to achieve, especially with children, in a capitalist, male-dominated society. And yet such relationships do exist, especially in subcultures which question traditional values. Some feminists would question this, for example, Paula Nicolson argues that the 'new man' has been shown to be a myth and that evidence demonstrates that men do not participate equally, especially in activities like taking time off work to care for a child who is ill. But my point is that although the non-traditional family does not represent the activities of most men, it is important to recognise the possibility of equal sharing of responsibility in the home by men and women (as well as same sex couples) and to see it as one possible vision of a more freeing family form which could grow, and be aimed for, in the future.

The importance of non-sexist attitudes

Although economics plays an important part, non-sexist attitudes toward family roles are essential in establishing a non-traditional family. These attitudes must then be translated into actions. Nowadays in traditional families men may feel obliged to 'help out' especially if the woman is employed. But this is a far cry from seeing the housework and child care, if children, as being as much his job as hers. In a non-traditional family instead of the woman doing a double shift, each partner does one and a half shifts. They share the burdens both of the inner world (at home) and the outer world (financial responsibility).

Although women are still disadvantaged in the job market, factors like male unemployment, the role of the welfare state in providing financial support and the growing power of women who are employed has led to a certain amount of financial equity in some families. But it is only through adopting non-sexist attitudes and actions that this financial equity can be translated into equal responsibility in the home.

Coming up against dominant values

The capitalist, male-dominated outer world doesn't always make it possible or advisable for both partners to work equally outside the home. Good child care is hard to find and women, especially with young children, may not be able to command a salary which is as high as the man. Women may want or need to spend more time with the children especially when they are young. And some women may not want to work in paid employment. So where does this leave the vision of a non-traditional family?

Without wanting to undermine the important work done by feminists which demonstrates how the vast majority of women are doing far more than their share of housework and child care, I wonder if the actual amount of work done by each partner in the home is the prime indicator we should use to define a relationship if, say, a man is working full time in the outer world and a woman is working full time in the home. Would we then ask if the man was actually doing his fair share by taking equal responsibility for the home when he's not working outside it? Other important questions in developing a non-traditional relationship are – does the woman have an equal amount of leisure time, spending money and decision-making power? This returns to the issue of non-sexist attitudes and actions by men in relationship to family roles. In other words, do both partners have an equal say in issues such as how and where the money is spent, the division of all household chores and child care (if children), the future direction of the family and leisure activities involving each partner having equal time for leisure? More important than what might be said, are their attitudes reflected in what actually happens?

Evidence of non-traditional families

The evidence I have of non-traditional families 'actually happening' is based on my own experience and observations, though I think it would be very useful for this to be followed up by more systematic sociological study. I have closely observed a variety of non-traditional families, with children, where the man and woman equally shared paid work and household work, where the woman was primarily responsible for paid work and the man for household work, where the man was employed full time and the woman part time and they shared household work and where a lesbian couple shared paid work and household work. In each of the families I've just mentioned there was a Jewish woman. I'm sure there are examples from other ethnic groups, particularly among lesbians.

My examples may be just a reflection of the people I know well, but it could also stem from the old tradition in the *shtetl* (the community in which Jews lived in Russia and Poland) of some housewives working outside the home, especially in the market-place. This happened particularly when men were scholars studying religious writings. Barbara Myerhoff points out that this public role was developed by women, but admired and accepted within the *shtetl*, even though it contrasted with the social ideal of the submissive wife and mother. It meant that women working outside the home had to be skilled at dealing with the outside community beyond the *shtetl* (often involving an excellent command of vernacular languages), the *shtetl* and the home. Negotiating her way through all these different realms took skill, energy and pragmatism.

Opening up debate

I'd like to open up a debate to examine and encourage non-traditional families. Certainly this must to be done in a way which doesn't undermine the struggle for public child care, wrongly assuming that the sharing of child care by some men would eliminate the need for public provisions. In fact, like other family forms, non-traditional families with children have a desperate need for child care. Another problem in discussing non-traditional families is that, in the past, the idea of symmetrical families has sometimes been used to cover over women's oppression.

The 'symmetrical family'

Some sociologists have used the term 'symmetrical families', to discuss nuclear family relationships which they saw as becoming partnerships between the men and women. Young and Willmott basically called a family symmetrical if the husband 'helped his wife' at least once a week. Such definitions exaggerate the number of nuclear families which do not fall into traditional roles and may be used to discredit feminist arguments about women's oppression in families. It is very important to be clear that the vast majority of women are still burdened with an unequal share of the housework and child care.

Women are still oppressed

Even in non-traditional families women are still oppressed by the expectations of male-dominated society and the effects of capitalism. But the non-traditional family can provide a vision of one kind of less oppressive family for women. In trying to develop a non-traditional family the internalised expectations not only of men, but of women feeling responsible for the housework and children, if any, have to be explored. We have grown up with the role models of our own mothers, as well as society's expectations. But in a non-traditional family we can hope that our children will be influenced by the fairer family role models we create.

A personal note

I remember my own confusion and nervousness about the family I was about to create in 1970 when I sat, pregnant, in the Chalk Farm Women's Consciousness Raising Group in London. What I saw as my particular solution was to become part of a nuclear family in which traditional male and female roles would not be played out. This 'experiment' seemed questionable at the time, though it is somewhat more common now.

Looking back on it, I think my husband and I did not understand the enormous influence the values of society would have on our children and ourselves. And yet we have somehow managed to share child care, housework (which often leads to a messy house) and financial responsibility. When the children were young this meant setting up a rota of working and watching the kids. We were often able to work at home which was very useful. Also at times we had outside child care and the help of grandparents. We were lucky to be able to manage this. Many couples with the same good intentions haven't been able to do so to as large an extent, although they've greatly altered the family roles they play. In the end I'd say changing those roles is most important.

Extended families

Classical

In a **classical extended family** relatives, beyond just parents and their children, live together. Classical extended families have often been seen to be more typical in peasant or pre-industrial societies. But this is not necessarily so. Families vary in different cultures. And within industrialised societies like Britain there are extended families. Among some ethnic groups like Asians, particularly Sikhs and East African Asians, there is a higher percentage of extended families. As there is no reason to see a classical extended family as having to stem from the base of a nuclear family, a household such as one with a grandmother, mother and her children living in Western industrial society also qualifies as a classical extended family.

Modified

In a more general way there are **modified extended families** where relatives who are not living together have regular contact with each other and act as some form of support network. People living in other types of families can also be seen as being a part of a modified extended family. Nowadays with telephones, cars and e-mail, family members can live far apart and still have regular contact with one another, providing emotional support and financial help when necessary.

Janet Finch has shown that a strong sense of obligation to relatives still exists in Britain. Government regulations (such as giving tax allowances if you support dependent relatives) and societal expectations that family members have a duty to help each other reinforces family ties. These expectations are gender-based, as there is a much stronger sense that women should help their relatives, especially parents and children. Government policy emphasising care in the community has increased the burden on women who care for elderly relatives or ill family members because insufficient resources are provided.

Collectively based families

Collectively based families are made up of at least some members who are not related, (or are not a couple) and are set up to create alternative families. They can take different forms. In Israeli kibbutzim children have been raised collectively, though they do spend time with their parents, and women are free to work outside the home. In the 1960s communes, which were often loosely based, blossomed. These had idealistic values, but didn't necessarily mean that women did less of the housework. But from the early 1970s feminists formed communes and collective households (which tended to be more well organised). These have provided valuable lessons and created positive living situations for some women and children. For example, Lynn Segal saw her collective household in the 1970s as providing ideal conditions for raising her son. And she has lived in collective households since then. Communes and collective households can set examples and create models for co-operative living. Other types of religious or utopian communities have existed for thousands of years and continue today.

Collectively based families have often been difficult to maintain over a long period of time because they tend to go against some of the dominant values in society. They have often been dismissed as unsuccessful, especially by traditionalists who find them threatening. But that is an over-simplification and some have lasted for many years.

Many young people, some with children, find communal living rewarding and/or financially useful. But, depending on the expectations and ideology of the members, they can also perpetuate hierarchical, male-dominated values where women end up doing a disproportionate amount of the housework. A commune or collective household can be a more freeing family form for women when it has been set up with a co-operative, non-sexist vision in which the members, especially the men, follow up their words with actions.

Couples without children are still a family

It is the expectation that married women are 'supposed' to have children that leads to the mistaken impression that a couple without children is somehow not a family. Again we see how the cereal-packet family image creates the idea that a women with a partner who doesn't have children is somehow lacking. This puts pressure on a woman with a sense that there are somehow unanswered questions about her.

Although there is a higher proportion of working women among couples without children, this does not automatically create a fair relationship, especially since women are disadvantaged in the job market. Just as with nuclear families, couples can be traditional or non-traditional depending on their gender expectations and actions. It often comes down to the same bottom line: is the man doing his fair share at home?

EXERCISE 7.1
Looking at your relationship to families

1 How would you describe your living situation? Do you live in a family? If so what kind of a family is it?
2 How would you describe your role in either or both the family you live in and/or your modified extended family, if you have one?
3 Is it possible to make your role in your family more freeing? If so, how?

Women's roles

Housewife–domestic worker

Whether or not a woman is living in a traditional nuclear family (and whatever else she may be doing) society's expectations are that she is responsible for the housework.

What exactly is housework?

At this point you may feel like sighing and saying that you know what housework is far too well. Although too many of us have more experience with housework than we'd like, taking a moment to step back and analyse it can be helpful in having a clearer picture of exactly what we do and how it fits into the larger issue of work. As anyone who's ever done housework knows, it certainly is work. And there's no other kind of work like it. It's the kind which is both unpaid, based on personal service and unlimited, leaving no guaranteed leisure. Housework is seen as a woman's occupation, with the word 'housewife' clearly specifying gender.

Ann Oakley divides housework into housework as work, which is often repetitive and unending, and 'the housewife role' which is more involved in caring for others and making a home. She suggests that the mixed feelings of many women toward housework involves their unhappiness with housework as work, rather than the caring 'housewife role' which is viewed more positively.

Studies on housework

In 1974 Ann Oakley did a classic feminist study called *The Sociology of Housework*. She talked to housewives in England and found that husbands helped more with child care than housework. But only a small number of husbands were giving the kind of help that could been seen as creating equality in marriage. In 1981 in the USA, Heidi Hartmann found no evidence of equal sharing of housework when hours spent on specific tasks were compared. In 1992 Fiona Devine studied the families of car workers in Luton, England, and found that although a larger number of women now worked part time, resulting in men helping out more with child care and a bit more with housework, women still remained responsible for these two areas. Studies show that traditional roles persisted even when men were unemployed.

Sexual division of labour

The **sexual division of labour** is work being divided along sexual lines. Traditionally, in our society, women's work has been seen to be in the home while men's work was in the outside, paid world. Nowadays large numbers of women work in paid employment. In the home we can see the sexual division of labour with most women responsible for the housework and child care. Even if men 'help out', women still do most of the housework.

There are many feminist debates in the area of sexual division of labour, looking at divisions based on gender in paid employment and the domestic sphere as well as the relationship between domestic and paid work. I have looked at some of these debates on housework in the section on differing feminist views of families. In the 1970s one strategy concerning housework was campaigning for 'wages for housework'. But this was criticised by other feminists who said it would keep women isolated in the low-paid, low-status area of domestic work.

EXERCISE 7.2 Look at your relationship to the sexual division of labour

1 Is there a sexual division of labour in your family, if you have one? (This could include your modified extended family.)
2 If there is a sexual division of labour, describe it. If not, describe how various forms of work are divided up.
3 Could the division of labour in your family be improved? If so, how?

Mothers and motherhood

I have written about how women are defined by motherhood and about psychological and social aspects of mothering in the section on *Women's Minds* in Chapter 6. You may find it helpful to go back and look at this before going on. Examining motherhood can be useful as it is one of society's prime expectations for women, but this is not meant to imply that women should be expected to have children or should be seen as 'abnormal' for not being mothers either by choice or from infertility.

The positive side of motherhood

Although society presents women with many problems in motherhood, being a mother can also be a wondrous experience which can be a positive part of a woman's identity. In 1983 Mary Boulton found that two-thirds of the mothers she interviewed felt that being a mother gave them meaning and purpose. I certainly would not have wanted to miss being a mother. Though there have been difficulties, my children have added a very special dimension to my life.

Diane Richardson in *Women, Motherhood and Childrearing* discusses how children can produce rewards for mothers in the form of insights, fun and extra vitality. She argues that it is not motherhood which feminists want to free women from, but the oppressive conditions they find in motherhood.

To make the experience of being a mother more enjoyable for those who want it, feminists have worked to give women the choice of whether or not to have children (through the right to contraception and abortion), tried to develop more freeing family forms, created support networks for mothers including refuges, worked to improve women's paid employment and maternity benefits, demanded that quality child care be available and worked for basic changes in society and its values.

Motherhood and the women's liberation movement

Sheila Rowbotham points out that as the Women's Liberation Movement began to bloom and mothers with young children voiced their complaints, it was important to oppose the myth of a woman's happiness and destiny being tied up in motherhood, which denied her other possibilities. Instead feminists said that being a mother had both an oppressive side and a fulfilling side, but that it needed to be socially transformed and freely chosen. They also made it clear that women had the right to be employed and be a mother, if they wanted, rather than having to choose between them. New kinds of relationships and social conditions were needed to do this in a more enriching way.

As time went on and second-wave feminists grew older many wanted children. But some women felt that the way the mystique of motherhood was being challenged left them feeling defensive. In the end there has been more of an acceptance of the complexities involved in motherhood.

Ann Oakley and motherhood

In *Taking it Like a Woman*, Ann Oakley describes her own depression as an isolated, exhausted mother with two young children living in a nuclear family in the late 1960s. She tells of her lack of social support and the lack of meaning in her life, though she loved her children dearly and was in what was considered a 'good' marriage. I was shocked by the dramatic contrast between her description and my vision of Ann Oakley as a highly competent, innovative researcher and writer. But it seems it was that conflict between her potential in the outer world and her complete confinement in the home which played an important role in her depression. She points out that she was not alone with most women in Britain depressed after childbirth and about a third of women depressed either most or some of the time.

Ann Oakley went on to gain insight from her own experiences and to use them to develop studies which would cast a new light on women's roles in families and motherhood. Her experiences can be a source of inspiration to help us move beyond our present feelings and experiences and use them as part of a force for positivity in the future.

Reproduction

Ann Oakley argues that although giving birth is a biological act, the culture in which a woman lives and society's view of women in general will define the meaning of childbirth. Both culture and society's attitudes toward women will reflect the economic system under which she lives. Because capitalism took most production out of the home, women's status was changed. And since there's a need for the production of new workers, women's role becomes reproduction rather than production. She sees a direct relationship between motherhood and economics; and the kind of motherhood we have in industrial society is unique in history.

Clearly reproduction, both in the sense of giving birth and raising the child, is labour. Anyone who's done it, or watched the process, knows it's hard work. Susan Himmelweit wants to end the social division between reproductive labour and production. This would ensure that our society stopped giving more social importance to producing things than producing people.

The institution of motherhood

In *Of Woman Born*, Adrienne Rich argues that the institution of motherhood is not the same as having children and caring for them. It is the institution of motherhood which demands that women be selfless, defining themselves in relation to others, instead of creating a sense of themselves. Oakley picks up on this idea defining the institution of motherhood as the way women in industrialised society become mothers. Although nowadays industrial society seems to be moving toward gender equality in jobs and education (the outer world), differences in the inner world of the home make external equality an illusion.

Transition to motherhood

Ann Oakley did a study in London of first-time mothers, *Becoming A Mother*, which showed the enormous impact on women's lives of the transition to motherhood. It brought massive changes in their lives. After the drama of birth itself, there are other major changes. New mothers give up paid work, (although some mothers return quickly to full-time employment, most wait and return later part time), become a housewife and take up the demanding career of motherhood. With isolated families and the institution of motherhood demanding women have 'maternal instinct' and focus on the needs of the baby rather than their own, there are enormous changes which involve rearranging one's identity. Motherhood often seems to lead to a lowered or 'depressed' sense of worth with children taking the spotlight and men advancing their careers.

Motherhood and difference

Our society views 'normal mothers' as being white, married and middle-class thus seeing other mothers as somehow 'abnormal' and lacking, which puts extra pressures on them. Beyond society's expectations, the experience of motherhood itself can differ depending on a woman's class, race, ethnicity and sexuality. This affects the social conditions of a woman being a mother. As Dosanj-Matwala and others point out, in Britain the experiences of some Asian women include arranged marriages, extended families and different relationships with husbands and children than most white middle-class women. In 1966 Hannah Gavron did ground-breaking research into the lives of mothers with young children, looking specifically at issues of class. She found that although both middle-class and working-class women lost independence when they became a mother, working-class women also had additional difficulties because of their lower income. Mary Boulton's study in 1983 supported her findings

Limitations of #'s position when became a mother

that the experiences of motherhood have a relationship to class. Although all the mothers she interviewed saw both positive and negative sides of mothering, more household space and modern conveniences (which middle-class mothers had) meant they could have a lighter burden. This gave them more time and space for other interests and reduced isolation.

Mother-blaming

Ann Wollett and Ann Phoenix point out that because psychological and child-care experts assume that mothers have the major, or even exclusive, responsibility for their children's development and behaviour, mothers are blamed when their children have problems or act in a way considered antisocial. They even see mother-blaming reflected in some feminists' views of their experiences of being a child in which their mothers are held responsible for their unhappiness in childhood, any disapproval mothers expressed and unhappiness in adulthood. It's as if mothers are the child's sole influence rather than fathers, schools or society being blamed. This leaves mothers in a 'no win' situation with mothers' experiences rarely being looked at from their internal perspective.

Sarah Ruddick and 'maternal thinking'

Sarah Ruddick argues that being a mother stimulates certain ways of looking at things and explaining the world, which she calls '**maternal thinking**'. This develops through the mother's experience of taking care of a child. The particular way of viewing things and being in the world that women develop to nurture children often involves taking on a style of 'cheerfulness' and 'humility'. Because of society's values and women's subordination this can be misconstrued as self-effacement and a kind of cheery denial. But Ruddick sees 'maternal thinking' as showing women's strength. Mothers need to be strong to deal with the social conditions of their role, involving many different activities, responsibilities and relationships. They also need to be strong to keep an identity of their own and take care of some of their own needs, while dealing with the social subordination of their role. She believes that having a feminist consciousness can help a woman be strong and clear in motherhood.

Motherhood as woman power

Being able to give birth to new life is a very powerful ability which women have and men have tried to control. The medicalisation of motherhood is an example of this, as male-dominated technology can be used to take control of the birth process from women when it is not necessary. When women do seek the use of technology such as in fertility treatment, unmarried women and lesbians are often assessed as 'abnormal'.

Some feminists celebrate motherhood as 'woman power', linking it to values of nurturing. Sheila Rowbotham criticises this approach, when used as a total political concept, because it confines women to the home, undermining working mothers and discounting the economic reality of many working-class and Black women who must balance low-paid jobs and child care. But she does see the power of motherhood as a partial acknowledgement of some women's experiences, at times, which could help to lead to more nurturing values in society.

If we look at the power women had during the period of goddess worship (see Chapter 2) we find women were not only held in high esteem for being able to give birth to new human life, but also for their work in growing plants for food.

The duality of power and submission

Sheila Rowbotham argues that when women try to decide whether or not to have children they see motherhood as involving power and submission linked together. Feminists basically think this complex linkage can be changed and are working to do this in various ways such as through psychoanalysis, different representations of motherhood, changing relationships and changing social conditions.

It is not motherhood itself, that is our biological ability to give birth, which is the problem; but the way the institution of motherhood is socially constructed in capitalist, male-dominated society.

Family issues

Child care – a woman's right

High-quality child care should be seen as a woman's right, rather than a privilege. A mother might choose not to use child care but it should be readily available, on demand, seen as a responsibility of the society. The Women's Liberation Movement demanded 24-hour child care. Some women do shift work or night work, while others want a space away from their children for leisure so that they can return to them fresher and with more energy. In a society which valued women and children, quality child care would be a readily available essential.

Child care helps families

Rather than child care working against maintaining families it helps to do so. A big stress in family life often revolves around child care. Both public and private child care tends not to have flexible hours for women to be able to drop children off early before work or pick them up late. So childminders, friends and relatives have to be relied on. Although these can be good situations, quality day care and before and after school care are in desperately short supply. The cost of child care is a major obstacle, keeping many mothers from being able to take up paid work. Single mothers on benefit are used as scapegoats when it is convenient, rather than being provided with the quality child care necessary for them to be able to be employed, if they choose.

Lack of child care reflects society's values

The lack of available, quality child care reflects our society's view of motherhood and families. During the Second World War when women were needed in the factories, child care was made available in countries such as Britain and the US and society did not frown on women for using it. Clearly, it is possible to create the kind of child care that women want and need, but in male-dominated, capitalist society this is generally not being done. Therefore, it has to be assumed that child care and the freedom it would give women is not seen as being in the interest of those with power in our society.

Feminists have been involved in working for high-quality, available child care for the last 25 years. Child care is not a petty issue which can be brushed aside, but one which would have a dramatic effect on women's lives and society as a whole.

EXERCISE 7.3 **Looking at your relationship to motherhood**

1 Think about why you did, do or don't want to have children.
2 How has your decision been affected by society's expectation of you as a woman?
3 If you are a mother how would your life be specifically changed by high quality, available child care? If you are not a mother how would the lives of mothers you know be changed?

Violence and power relationships

In this subsection I will be focusing on male violence, in the form of battering, and how it affects power relationships in families. For a discussion of male violence and the different feminist perspectives on it, as well as rape, see Chapter 5. For a discussion of the psychological affects of violence against women see Chapter 6 and for sexual harassment see Chapter 8.

Battering

Battering is the physical abuse of a woman by her male partner, such as beating and rape. A man battering a woman is the most extreme demonstration of male power in relationships. Too often it has, historically and culturally, been seen as acceptable.

Feminists have played a leading role in bringing the issue of battering to the forefront and demanding changes. Battering is far too commonplace. Feminists have worked to protect and empower women by creating refuges for battered women and their children. They have tried to change the law and make sure that existing laws are enforced. They have also looked at the root causes of male violence and worked to change them.

An extension of power relationships

Feminists have differing views on the exact nature of the root causes of male violence. However, they take the same basic approach in believing that society must recognise that the battering of a woman can never be seen as a private matter, but must be viewed as a social problem which cannot be allowed to continue. In other words, the beating or rape of a woman by her partner can only be understood by looking at it in a social context. Then we see that the battering of a woman is an extension of the power relationships within male-dominated families and within society as a whole.

Michele Bograd argues in *Feminist Perspectives on Wife Abuse* that male violence, or the threat of it, has been used to keep men powerful in the family; although there are other ways used to keep women submissive, male violence is the most effective way of maintaining social control. Even if individual men aren't violent themselves, she sees them benefiting as a group from women being limited by their fear of battering or male violence in general. Battering reinforces women being passive and men having the 'right' to be in control.

Feminists have looked at what function the battering of women serves within specific societies and historical times. A number of feminists have argued that this must be done with an understanding of other power relationships such as class and race.

The importance of women's refuges

Since the 1970s feminists have operated refuges for women and their children to live in to escape attack. These are open to all women. They not only provide accommodation and security from their violent partner, but also give women a chance to get beyond their own isolation and come to see that their experiences have not taken place because of their own personal failure.

Refuges have not only demonstrated the seriousness of women's suffering, but the difficulties women have because of the housing situation, societal values and the law in escaping violent partners. (I have discussed the psychological problems involved in leaving a violent partner in Chapter 6 and have given the address for Women's Aid refuges in the appendix.)

Women's Aid has played a leading role in bringing the issue of battering into the open and demanding changes in social structure, laws and personal attitudes to end battering. But Val Binney points out that the long-term success of the feminist attack on battering lies in its ability to keep the issue alive as an unsolved problem. This involves insisting on battering being understood, not simply through a psychiatric explanation, but as women's powerlessness within the family.

EXERCISE 7.4 Looking at violence against women

1 How have you been affected, either directly or indirectly, by battering and/or male violence in general?
2 What do you think should be done to end violence against women?
3 What long-term and short-term strategies would you set up to achieve this?

The role of the state in families

Marriage

Although marriage is seen in our society as a very private relationship, the fact that it is controlled by the state shows that it has a much wider significance. Stevi Jackson argues that marriage is the state-sanctioned institution which puts many women into an unequal relationship with men. Although she sees men directly benefiting, she doesn't believe this unequal relationship is in-built between men and women, but is connected to the larger economic and social structure.

Historically marriage in Britain was a patriarchal institution in which a man had enormous legal powers over his wife including her property, children, labour power and the authority to 'chastise' her (see Chapter 2).

Stevi Jackson points out that although men now have less power, marriage is still not an equal relationship. Formal, legal equality has no meaning so long as women are not economically equal and other state agencies reinforce inequality. Even the definition of equality is based on male ideas. Women have been given child custody not as a right, but because of their role in the family so long as they are seen to be a 'good' mother. Although British law concerning marriage and divorce has moved toward greater formal equality, this has not always been in women's interests and legal processes keep re-creating male-dominated relationships.

The state doesn't only regulate family life, it actually defines what counts as a family. In Britain we can see this in regulations concerning the need for a woman to have a father for her child to get infertility treatment. Because marriage is defined as heterosexual, lesbian couples are seen as a 'deviant' family form and are not allowed to legally marry. Also a lesbian partner does not automatically have any legal relationship with the children she has helped to raise.

In Britain there is a trend away from marriage, although most women marry at least once in their lives. More women are staying single, not having children or having them outside marriage. More women are living with men without getting married. And it is becoming the norm to live together before getting married. Yet this trend must be seen in perspective as living together may not necessarily make much difference in gender roles. Also divorce rates in Britain, Europe and the US have been rising steadily.

Welfare
Fran Bennett points out that the British welfare state operates with

underlying assumptions about female roles in families. A woman is supposed to be economically dependent on any man she lives with, but she does not have the right of access to a man's income from wages or benefits. Women are supposed to care for dependants, which can include elderly and disabled relatives as well as their own children. It is assumed that they will do this in private with not much help. Provisions for families depend mostly on the welfare state's view of women's roles.

Welfare and families are often seen as 'women's issues', which creates a dilemma for feminists. On one hand, we know how important issues of welfare are to women's lives (especially women pensioners and single mothers on benefits), though information about welfare issues are often put together in such a way as to make women invisible or lumped together with families. An example of this is using the term 'single families' when nine out of ten of them in Britain are headed by women. But while we want to show how women are disadvantaged, we don't want welfare provisions to be seen as 'just a women's issue'. This would mean them being pushed to one side and not taken seriously as an important political and economic concern.

Bennett argues that despite the complexities, feminists have created some guiding principles on welfare. Within a larger strategy feminists demand an independent income for women, which would recognise the value of domestic work without either encouraging full-time housework or penalising women who take part in paid employment. The benefits system must generally encourage social and economic changes in relationships of power between the sexes and specifically encourage changes in the sexual division of labour. The state should also compensate women for continued inequalities, where it is necessary.

State regulation and reproductive choice

State regulation of a woman's reproduction not only affects her own right to self-control of her body, but the establishment of families and a woman's role within them. In other words, without reproductive control a woman can be taken over by her family. Keeping women in 'their place' has been a goal of family traditionalists who have been able to affect the state. A clear example of this is the struggle to maintain abortion rights in the US. Connie Paige points out that various groups of family traditionalists, brought together by the New Right, campaigned to pressure the state to take back the rights women had won to control their ability to become mothers and establish families by being able to choose whether or not to have an abortion. The American Right has used the issue of a woman's right to choose to gain political power at the expense of women who have been forced to have children whom they cannot properly care for. Ironically, they have then turned round and blamed single mothers for being dependent on government money.

Denise Riley points out that the right to choose means that women must be able to decide to have children as well as not to. But for that choice to actually be freely made there must be provisions for quality housing, jobs and child care.

EXERCISE 7.5

1 How have you been affected by the role of the state on issues of marriage, welfare and reproductive choice?
2 What role do you think the state should play regarding families?
3 Have your views and/or expectations of your family, if you have one, been changed by reading this? If so, how?

8

EMPLOYMENT

Can't seem to get away from work. At home and outside, it follows me about. Can't live without work, especially 'cause it pays the bills. No matter how sick of work I get, it gives my life meaning. Still, I wouldn't mind unwinding on a sunny beach. Then I'd come back, clear headed, to all my various forms of work.

What is work?

What work is depends on how you look at things

From a woman's point of view housework is clearly never-ending work (see Chapter 7). And yet from our society's view nothing counts as work unless you're paid for it. As Linda McDowell and Rosemary Pringle point out in *Defining Women*, Western, male-dominated society sees work and home as opposites. Home is given the 'feminine' qualities of caring in a personal setting, while work is seen as the 'masculine' sphere of order and rationality. But that, of course, is looking at it from a male point of view. Women often find their home anything but a place where they are cared for and can relax. For them it is generally a place of work (whether or not they're in employment). It is in the home where they are trying to create order and may even find employment relaxing in the sense of being able to get away from the demands of the children and household. Sometimes the home is also a place where women are their husband's unpaid secretaries. So for women the home is generally a place of work.

History

This division between home and work did not exist in Western, pre-industrial society as work of all kinds was mostly done around households (see Chapter 5). Work was not defined as earning money through outside employment. It wasn't until the nineteenth century that people became consumers who went out and spent money, which was earned through employment, to buy most of what they needed. Before that although, at times, most households had some kind of an outside income in England, it was not their mainstay. Being waged full time was often looked down upon not only because a person lost their independence, but because it didn't provide security the way things like growing food at home did. In fact, women were often the ones who earned most of the money by selling some of what was grown in the market place and later by making textile goods at home. Seeing work as something that is done by a male breadwinner, who goes out and brings home a family wage, only developed in the nineteenth century. But Harriet Bradley points out in *Men's Work, Women's Work* that patterns of segregation of the kinds of work done by men and women goes back to pre-industrial societies.

Pre-industrial societies
Looking at the ways in which work was divided along sexual lines in various pre-industrial societies, it becomes clear (through evidence from anthropologists and historians) that there was an almost unending variety of forms that this division took. Just about every activity was, at some time in some place, seen as 'women's work'. Still, there were general patterns which were more common. 'Men's work' was most often seen as hunting large animals, metalwork, fishing, mining and lumberwork. 'Women's work' was not so clearly defined. But tasks done mostly by women have been generally described as providing for food; caring for the home, children and the sick; teaching and making clothes. These have often been done by women in homes. They are linked to what is seen in industrial societies as 'domestic' tasks, which are either unpaid housework or low-paid labour.

When women go out in the labour market they often do paid versions of these same tasks which focus around care and servicing of people. Today in many parts of the world large numbers of women are nurses, teachers, garment workers and cleaners, while other jobs are associated with beauty and glamour. Bradley sees this coming about through sex-typing. **Sex-typing** is the process by which jobs are assigned to a particular sex. It is the idea behind seeing tasks as 'women's work' or 'men's work'.

Different definitions of work
Work is defined differently depending on your societal point of view, the time you're living in and your culture. In this way what is defined as work can be seen to be not essentially the same to everyone but socially constructed.

Fine, fine but what are you calling work?

At this point I can just hear you saying that even if what's seen as work changes we still can't go on without saying what it is. Certainly I feel that way, so I'm using the definition of work as being the production of goods and services. This clearly includes housework which is discussed in detail in Chapter 7.

Why study employment?

To be able to find a job, get a better one or have an easier time in the one you have, it's important to know as much as you can about that beast we call employment. It helps to understand what happens to women in paid work and why. Maybe you're stuck in a low-paying job or trapped on a low grade. The cards are often stacked against us. If we want to change that we have to be ahead of the game enough to know what's really going on and what we can do about it. Whatever your relationship to paid work, by finding out more about the ideas behind it you have a better chance of figuring out how best to deal with employment.

EXERCISE 8.1 **Looking at work**

1 Make a list of all the different kinds of work (unpaid and paid) which you do.
2 Try keeping track of how much time you spend working during the period of a week. Now look at how much you were paid for your work.

Discrimination in employment

Gender discrimination

As the Equal Opportunities Commission's booklet, 'Women and men in Britain 1995', points out, in general, women in Britain are in a worse economic position than men of a similar age all through their lives. Whether or not they are employed, women have lower incomes than equivalent men. In employment, women often work in different types of jobs than men. They are more likely to go into clerical/secretarial, service and sales jobs. These areas of employment are associated with part-time hours. If women have children they generally need to work part time because there is a serious shortage of child-care places for under-fives. The places which do exist usually don't provide enough hours of care for full-time work. Also some women want to work less hours to have more time with their children.

In higher-level jobs, with higher pay, such as professionals and managers, few women work part time. This causes problem for mothers. Clearly, having dependent children lessens a woman's economic activity. This is demonstrated by the fact that women between the ages of 20 and 40 without children have a similar pattern of employment to men.

A marked difference between the incomes of women and men in Britain is shown after the age of 65. Women over the age of 65 have lower levels of income than men. UK figures from the mid-1990s show that between the ages of 65 and 74 there is a dramatic difference in income between the sexes with women getting an average of £96 a week and men getting £182 per week. This is because men get three times as much in private or occupational pensions than women, as well as 37 per cent higher state pensions and more state benefits than women.

Women often take time from paid work to care for children and relatives at home. Not only does this give them a lower income at the time, but it seriously lowers their income when they are older. Women are discriminated against for doing the caring, unpaid work which society expects and needs them to do. One way in which the state maintains this discrimination is by not providing the needed quality child care.

Racial discrimination

Women don't only find themselves discriminated against in employment as a result of their gender. Because of racist attitudes and expectations in society it can be more difficult for Black women to get jobs. This means they have a greater chance of ending up in low-paying, low-status jobs. One study (by Jenkins in 1986) of managers and personnel officers in a bank in Britain found that when Black candidates had the skills and qualifications needed for a job they were often considered 'unacceptable' because of expectations that they would not fit in or because of how white managers judged their manner, appearance or attitude. Retail firms were also less likely than the public sector to advertise posts openly.

Because it can be harder for Black women to get jobs it is not surprising that in Britain there is a higher percentage of Black women who are unemployed than white women, according to the Labour Force Survey of 1990–91. At every qualification level Black people have higher levels of unemployment than whites. Although Black women face more discrimination, there are many successful Black women in employment and self-employment.

Class discrimination

As well as discrimination based on gender and race, many Black and white women are held back because they are working class. Economic power plays an important role in our society and women find themselves in different relationships to it. This affects many aspects of their lives from their education to their income. In employment, working-class women are disadvantaged both by their class and gender. This translates into low-paying, low-status jobs.

Lindsay German argues for a class analysis of women's oppression. She sees it as in the interests of both working-class women and men to fight to overturn the society which exploits them and therefore to fight for women's liberation. She also sees it in the interest of the capitalist class to have labour power reproduced privately at home where women are unpaid and to have women paid low wages for outside work. Although this leads to unequal family relationships, she does not see this as benefiting men because all family members would be better off in a society where relationships weren't straitjacketed.

Disability and employment discrimination

Women with disabilities are discriminated against in employment. As Susan Lonsdale points out in *Women and Disability* both in Britain and the US only 29 per cent of women with disabilities are employed. In each country there is a higher percentage of both men with disabilities and able-bodied women who are employed, while able-bodied men have the highest percentages of employment. Black and/or working-class women with disabilities have even more difficulties. Unemployment makes it harder for women with disabilities to be independent because of lack of adequate income. It also means they may not have the social relations and daily structure which outside paid work provides. This can contribute to women with disabilities being lonely and losing confidence.

When women with disabilities do find paid work, there is a greater chance that they will end up in low-skilled jobs. In Britain there is a larger proportion of women with disabilities who are in unskilled work than either men with disabilities or able-bodied women. Studies have shown that when women become disabled they face downward mobility and unemployment. But there are also successful employed and self-employed women with disabilities.

Although not all women with disabilities want or need to be employed for fewer hours, some do. This may either be because they are bringing up children or it may relate to their disability. But appropriate part-time work is hard to find. And in Britain there is also the problem of part-time work disqualifying them for certain social security benefits. This not only keeps many women with disabilities dependent on the state, when they'd like to work part time, but also makes it more difficult for them to integrate into everyday life.

Discrimination based on sexual orientation

Marny Hall points out that because many lesbian workers have had such painful, negative experiences when they revealed their sexual orientation (including losing jobs, promotions or projects) many conceal the fact that they're lesbian from their co-workers and employers. But non-disclosure has its own problems. Not only does it put a barrier between a woman's life in employment and leisure time, but it means she must be on guard against her 'secret' getting out. In order to cope lesbians adopt a number of strategies. These include avoidance of personal interactions at their jobs, conveying an image of differentness which is focused on being a progressive feminist instead of a lesbian, partial disclosure to those at work who can be trusted and using 'he' instead of 'she' when discussing their partner. Non-disclosure puts a lesbian in a difficult moral position, but many women working in corporations see no other choice.

Some lesbians who have come out feel that they are set up as the token lesbian and still haven't been able to be themselves. Others have felt that being lesbian has given them a sense of strength and confidence. Being seen as unmarried or, in the case of some women, more masculine has sometimes meant they've been given more challenging assignments.

Employment organisation and gender

In order to more specifically understand how women are held back in employment, we will look at how paid work is organised and how this affects women.

Job segregation

Job segregation by gender is the way women and men are separated into different types of paid work. This often means they are not competing for the same jobs. Segregation is a major cause of lower pay for women. They tend to be paid less, even when they do the same types of work as men. There are two kinds of job segregation.

In **horizontal segregation** women and men have different jobs in different workplaces. Some jobs are seen as 'men's work', like coal mining, and others are considered 'women's work', such as being a school dinnerlady. The jobs that women do are often an extension of the unpaid, caring work they do at home. Comparatively less men do these jobs while men as a whole have a far wider range of paid work.

In **vertical segregation**, women and men basically do the same types of work but women are mostly found in the lower-paid positions which are seen to be less skilled and responsible. In this way women speak of the **glass ceiling** – not being given an equal opportunity to rise beyond a certain level into higher jobs. An example of this in Britain, in 1993, was that 48 per cent of secondary school teachers were women while only 20 per cent of headteachers were women, according to the Equal Opportunities Commission.

Changes in employment

Technology, skill and deskilling

Technology has been seen to bring about **deskilling**. This is because assembly lines such as the ones started by Henry Ford in the United States meant that each worker put the same part on lots of different cars, rather than knowing how to build a car or even understanding how it worked. Deskilling gives workers less control and managers more.

Veronica Beechey points out that women are especially vulnerable to deskilling because they have less chance of being unionised and because employers have used gender divisions to deskill jobs by replacing men who are higher paid and are seen to be skilled workers, with lower-paid women who are seen to be less skilled. She argues that the whole concept of skill is socially constructed. When women do jobs that need skills, such as cooking or cleaning, they're often said to be unskilled or semi-skilled workers. Women's skills in areas such as cooking and cleaning are devalued both because they are seen as 'women's work' and because there are many women who have these skills. Men are often better organised in unions and can better protect their jobs which are considered to be more highly skilled 'men's work'.

Computers and deskilling of women clerks

Computers can make it easier for tasks to be very specialised, deskilling workers. This can particularly affect women. For example, in a study of the operation of a bank it was found that most women were in the lowest two grades of clerical work. This involved them following highly specified procedures to put data into the computer and work as cashiers. The higher grades of clerks were doing more complex work and some grades included limited managerial responsibility. Only the higher-level staff actually used the information on the computers for their work. Since computerisation the job of each grade of clerk has been made very specific, while before computerisation each clerk did a wider range of tasks based on their age and experience.

Women and the flexible workforce

In the late twentieth century the labour market in industrialised countries has been seen to become more flexible. We are said to have come into a Post-Fordist or Neo-Fordist era with more small scale, flexible production. This is generally described as involving a **core workforce** of full-timers, with better pay and working conditions, which is supplemented by lots of **peripheral workers** who are temporary, part time or subcontracted.

Sylvia Walby argues that we must look at how this affects women. There are some areas, like clerical work, where women would be a good part of the core workforce. But the growth of part-time female paid work is a strategy by employers to more effectively exploit women workers. Although these peripheral workers create profitable flexibility for employers the women get less pay and protection in their jobs.

Some feminists argue that there is basically nothing new in the way women are being treated; for a long time women have been used as a **reserve labour force**, being hired by employers to only work when and how they are needed.

Issues in employment equality

Employment equality and the law

The law can be an important vehicle in moving toward equality, but it needs to be seen in perspective. Laws often come about through mass campaigns and actions. They need to be part of a larger change in attitudes and unequal structures. Also laws are not always followed or acted upon even-handedly in a society with unequal power relationships.

In Britain the Equal Pay and Sex Discrimination Acts came into effect in 1975. They were supposed to ensure the rights of women to equal opportunities. The Equal Pay Act made it illegal for women to get a lower rate of pay than men if they did the same work for the same employer in the same place or if they did work which was considered broadly similar or was given an equal rating.

The issue of what jobs are judged to have equal value or comparable worth is important to women and there have been a number of test cases and some important victories. In Britain many groups such as the Low Pay Unit advise women to put in equal pay claims. Although this can be useful, some feminists argue that judgments of whether jobs have comparable worth too often reflect the values of male-dominated society. For example, job evaluation schemes have tended to highly value physical strength. So male supermarket storeroom workers were given a higher grade than predominately female cashiers, even though they were responsible for handling the money. Grading systems such as this have often meant women ended up in lower grades, which didn't take account of their skills. Some companies have also moved certain jobs to make pay comparisons impossible. These actions, plus the fact that 'women's work' is often done in a different place than 'men's work', has meant that although the Equal Pay Act may have helped to lessen the difference between male and female pay, many women still get paid far less than men. European legislation has helped to improve conditions for women workers in Britain, but there are still many problems. If Britain had not opted out of the European Social Chapter, working conditions for women would have been somewhat improved.

The gender pay gap

The gender pay gap demonstrates how women are undervalued and treated unequally. In Britain the Equal Opportunities Commission, which was set up to enforce the Equal Pay and Sex Discrimination Acts, points out that a gender pay gap still exists although there has been progress. In 1975 women's average hourly wage was less than three-quarters that of men. In 1996 they reported that women still only get four-fifths of men's average hourly wage. There is even a greater difference when part-time workers are examined. Almost half of women employees work part time and get paid less than 60 per cent of the average hourly wage of men working full time.

Low pay

Low pay affects women's quality of life and ability to be independent. Not only does it mean that women cannot afford to buy things that they and their children need or want, but it can often trap women and their children in a cycle which limits their physical and social mobility. It also affects how women are viewed socially. In a capitalist society, pay and the consumer goods it can or can't buy are an indicator of social status. In other words, women are undervalued even though between the home and employment they work more hours than men and provide services which are essential to society. People who care for money, such as predominately male financial and property managers, get paid far more than women who care for people. And in private industry it is those who receive the profits who benefit from women's low pay.

The Low Pay Unit points out that in Britain in the mid-1990s, women are twice as likely as men to be low paid, with 800,000 women earning less than £2.50 an hour and homeworkers making as little as 50 pence an hour. Weekly averages show that women hairdressers, bar staff, laundry workers, cleaners, and sales checkout assistants earn less than men doing the same jobs.

Homeworking

Too often the only way women can 'fit in' work around their children is to work part time for low pay or become involved in **homeworking** which for women often involves piece-work and low pay. Although, at the moment, homeworking can be a better-than-nothing option both for women with disabilities and those with young children, it is isolating, undervaluing and can present health problems for these women and their families.

Many homeworkers have no written contracts and receive irregular pay based on piece-work rates and work availability. Most homeworkers receive no sick pay, holiday pay, maternity pay or pensions. They have little chance for training to break out of the homeworking cycle. In Britain the National Group on Homeworking has been set up to try to improve the rights of homeworkers.

Stuck at the bottom

Another important issue around working conditions for women is getting stuck in low-grade jobs. This may happen because women's skills are not recognised, because training is not available to them or because women can face poor promotion prospects. Of course, this can bring us back to the same vicious circle as women's prospects of promotion can be hampered by the fact that they have to work part time because of lack of adequate child care.

EXERCISE 8.2 Looking at employment issues

1 In what ways have you been discriminated against or ill-treated in employment, either presently or in the past?
2 How would you describe and classify these?
3 What demands would you make for better treatment?

Demands towards equality

Women in paid work have raised a series of issues and demands to improve their lives. There are discussions below about specific concerns such as child care. But there are also more general issues involving the changing of profit-orientated, male-dominated attitudes. Some feminists argue that the structure of society which has created these attitudes and economic and political power relationships needs to be changed.

Child care

For women with children it is essential to have someone to care for the youngsters in order to do paid work. Because the number of hours of child care are usually limited, women must structure their employment around their children's hours at day care or school. The lack of quality, affordable child care puts an enormous amount of pressure on women.

Far more quality, affordable child care, especially for under-fives, is needed in countries such as Britain, the US and Canada. It should be provided at the place of employment. Child care must be available during all the hours that it is needed and should be seen as a woman's right rather than a privilege. (See the section on child care in Chapter 7 for more details.)

Equal treatment of part-timers

One important demand is for equal treatment of part-time workers, who are often predominantly women. This involves giving them hourly rates equivalent to full-timers, entitlements like sick pay, pensions and holiday pay on the same basis as full-timers, job security and the same chances for training and promotion. In Britain the European Equal Treatment Directive gave part-time workers almost the same rights as full-time workers. Although this has created improvements, part-time women workers are still often low-paid and more exploited than full-timers.

Job sharing

One way to give part-timers all the rights and pay of full-timers is through job sharing. **Job sharing** is where a full-time job is shared between people. They should each get the benefits of a full-time job and not be pressured into working more hours than has been agreed.

There can be many variations of job sharing. For example, there are a number of half time appointments for lecturers at further and higher education colleges. This gives these lecturers all the benefits of a full-time appointment while the college gets lecturers with the added perspective and energy of a member of staff who isn't there on a daily basis. Other variations involve doing paid work three days a week or four days a week.

A minimum wage, set at a reasonable level

A minimum wage must be set at a reasonable level of pay so that women are not forced to live in poverty. In countries such as Britain, where it does not presently exist, a minimum wage needs to be instituted and set at a reasonable standard. This would raise the wages of the lowest-paid workers, many of whom are women living in poverty. It would also make it possible for some women living on benefits to become employed and be able to afford the necessary child care.

Expanded training and education for women

As discussed in other chapters, historically women have suffered from lack of access to education as well as gender stereotyped, inferior education. This has not only limited their job possibilities, but has affected their whole lives.

Training and education for women needs to be greatly expanded to widen their horizons beyond sex-stereotyped occupations and expectations. Although there have been some improvements there's still a long way to go. For example, training women to use computers for more complex tasks could help them move beyond the lowest grades of clerks which many women now find themselves stuck in. Even with the limited expectations for women in our society, the skills they've often developed match well with those needed for using computers. First, women often have good communication and keyboard skills. Second, much of what many women do in taking care of a family involves problem solving, which is so basic to computer applications and programming. Other necessary qualities in computing, which women have often developed, are patience and persistence. It's that male-dominated mystique of computers (such as all those computer games where male heroes fight their way through to save the helpless, screaming princess) which both makes computers seem alien to some women and helps preserve male access to them. The field of computing involves skills which are not based on physical strength and it builds on the expertise that many women have already developed. Therefore, it could be a field in which more women excelled if they were given training, support and access to equipment.

EXERCISE 8.3 **Following up on demands**

1 How could you follow up on demands you may have concerning employment?
2 What specifically could be done?
3 From what groups or individuals could you receive information or support?

Health and safety

Health and safety is an important issue for everyone at home and in employment. But there are aspects of health and safety in paid work which generally affect women either because of the kinds of jobs they tend to do or because of reproductive issues.

Reproductive issues

Pregnant workers and women workers who may someday have children not only contribute the value of their own labour, but also the value of future workers through their ability to reproduce. Women's reproductive contribution (if they have children) benefits society. Therefore, it is in the interest of society, not just pregnant women, to be concerned about reproductive health and safety in employment. When we look at it this way it is very different than the perspective often presented in male-dominated, capitalist society where it is seen as necessary to restrict women because they might get pregnant. Besides, all workers have the right to health and safety and unsafe exposure by male workers to certain chemicals, physical agents and machinery can also harm their offspring.

Maternity rights not privileges

It is not a privilege but a right of pregnant workers and new mothers to have protection and maternity benefits. In countries such as Britain women have gained some recognition of their maternity rights. These generally include maternity leave with benefits like holiday time and pension rights maintained; maternity pay; the right not to be dismissed and to return to their old job or, if necessary, an equivalent one; the right not to be refused a job because of future consequences of a woman being pregnant; the right to paid time off for ante-natal care and protection against health and safety risks for pregnant workers and breastfeeding mothers. Not all women in Britain receive all the rights mentioned above, although European Community rulings have generally improved maternity rights in Britain.

Chemical exposure

Women can suffer from an unsafe chemical exposure. Beyond more generalised problems these difficulties can include infertility, menstrual disturbances and genetic damage which can cause birth defects. An unsafe chemical exposure can affect reproductive health before and after a baby is conceived.

Employers are obliged to do assessments of chemical risks and have safety procedures. But this does not always happen since too often profits are their main concern. It is important to remember that when trying to find out about the true hazards of chemicals do not only rely on information from suppliers or manufacturers, who again are often more concerned about profits. Union health and safety representatives can play an important role. Independent sources of information should be used. For example, in Britain there is the London Hazards Centre. Workers should demand that tests for exposure to known or suspected reproductive and/or other toxins be provided.

Physical agents – VDU work

Many women do work involving a computer visual display unit (VDU). This may cause difficulties if health and safety procedures are not followed. General recommendations related to VDU work include regular breaks away from the screen (10 minutes every hour), sitting as far away from the screen as is comfortable and avoiding working more than half the day at the VDU, if possible. Repetitive strain injury (RSI) is an occupational illness which women VDU users should also be aware of and employers should assess risks. As well as following the suggestions above, workers who are using keyboards should have enough space for support of hands and arms and to change position and vary movements. They also need an adjustable, ergonomic work-chair.

During pregnancy, some physical agents (such as X-rays) are known to be hazardous, while others are suspected. The issue of whether working with a VDU increases the risk of miscarriage or birth defects is undecided. But some studies show that using a VDU for more than 20 hours a week during the first three months of pregnancy or exposure to VDUs with a high level of extremely low frequency (ELF) magnetic fields in early pregnancy increases the risk of miscarriage. Other related factors may be poor work-station ergonomics and stress at work. Some unions in Britain have negotiated the right of workers who are pregnant or trying to become pregnant to transfer to non-VDU work, if they wish.

Black and ethnic minority women face more hazards

Research has shown that Black and ethnic minority workers in industrial nations such as Britain face increased risks of occupational accidents, injuries and diseases. This is because many of them are in low-paying jobs with poor working conditions. Often there is no occupational health provision. There is a lack of health and safety enforcement in places such as sweat shops or small companies or for homeworkers. Racism and sexism team up to put Black and ethnic minority women in positions where it is hard for them to refuse to do hazardous work.

Stress

Although stress is not a disease, it can cause many illnesses. Symptoms associated with stress-related illnesses include insomnia, headaches, indigestion, muscle cramps and aches, fatigue, not being able to concentrate, depression, tension, impulsive and hostile behaviour and/or irregular periods. In *Women at Work*, Deborah Clarke defines **stress** as high demands coupled with high constraints and low support.

Although stress affects both men and women there are some factors which can make stress more acute for women. These include low-paid jobs with less security, status and control combined with domestic responsibilities. The double shift of many women, at home and at a job, means they often labour for very long hours pressured by responsibilities, monetary problems and tight deadlines rushing between their jobs and picking up children or elderly dependants. It is their lack of support alongside high demands and tight constraints which can cause stress. Some feminists argue that the root cause of these problems are our capitalist, male-dominated society.

Coping with stress

Getting more support can help with stress. This might involve anything from demanding more help from a partner, if any, to getting more support at work from colleagues or a union.

It can be helpful to be caring and gentle with yourself. Identify where stress is coming from and then try to develop constructive strategies to deal with it. Build a positive support network. Acknowledge your feelings and share them with your support network. Plan your time and try to develop a sense of direction and purpose. Be clear about your own limits and learn to say 'No'.

Assertiveness

Assertiveness can be not only empowering, but can also be helpful in dealing with stress. Too often women find themselves caught in situations where it seems to them they don't have any power while they're getting the brunt of the anger or pressure from others, often men. **Assertiveness** is expressing and acting on one's own needs and feelings in a direct, honest way which is not punishing to others. It means standing up for your rights without violating the rights of others.

Assertiveness is the more effective way between passiveness and aggressiveness. Too often women have been raised to be passive, giving in to the needs of others while finding it hard to stand up for themselves. This can lead to feeling powerless and depressed. On the other hand, women who find it hard to assert themselves may hold in their feelings of frustration, hurt and injustice until they explode into aggressiveness. Aggression violates the rights of others as well as being ineffective in creating a positive, co-operative atmosphere.

Know your rights
In becoming more assertive it is helpful to begin to develop a sense of yourself as a person who has rights. You may find it helpful to be clear about your general rights at work by talking to a union or support organisation. Then try thinking about your own individual rights. Deborah Clarke suggests that as a woman you have a right to state your own wants, needs, priorities, feelings, opinions and values. You have the right to be treated with respect as an intelligent, capable person who can make mistakes, change their mind or even be uncertain. You have the right to decide not to take responsibility for other people's problems, deal with people without being dependent on their approval and generally to say 'yes' or 'no' for yourself.

Assertiveness techniques
As Deborah Clarke points out, there are a number of assertiveness techniques which are useful in employment.

Broken record   Begin by being sure in your own mind about what you feel and want. Then turn it into a clear statement like, 'I can't work overtime this week.' Now no matter what the other person says to you keep repeating your statement. There's no need to get into an argument with them or be distracted by anything they say, just calmly stick with your truth: 'I won't be able to work overtime this week.'

Saying, 'NO'   Many women find it hard to say, 'no', because it's not pleasing to others, but this means they find themselves taking on more than they can handle. If this is a problem for you try practising saying 'No', without apology or aggression. You can do this in front of the mirror or with a friend. If you're not sure whether or not you can or want to do something when you are asked, request some time to think it over.

Body language   Use posture, voice and eye contact to be assertive. You can practise this by looking in the mirror. Observe the look on your face as you practise being assertive with someone at work. Think of what kind of clothing you can wear which will add to your confidence.

EXERCISE 8.4 **Developing assertiveness**

1   Think about your own rights. Try writing something about them. You may want to talk about general areas as mentioned above and/or write about your rights in specific situations in which you find yourself. How can you use your rights in an assertive way?
2   Look at the way you deal with people and situations. Without being down on yourself, try to see if you are passive, aggressive or assertive in each instance.
3   Think about your friends, relatives and workmates, if any. Do they tend to be passive, aggressive or assertive in their relationship to you and other people?
4   Can you think of a situation in which one of the assertiveness techniques described above could be especially useful? How would you specifically use it?

Sexual harassment

Sexual harassment involves a number of different forms of unwanted sexual attention like leering; unwanted sexual jokes, teasing, comments or questions; unwanted pressure for sexual favours which can have implied threats for not co-operating; unwanted touching or pinching and/or assault. Sexual harassment at work is a serious problem which many women have experienced. In *Intimate Intrusions*, Elizabeth A. Stanko argues that often women can be just as upset by persistent harassment which is considered 'low level', like leering and sexual comments, as by the more physical type of touching and pinching.

When subjected to sexual harassment on a daily or regular basis the effects mount up. Women have reported feeling humiliated, nervous, threatened and helpless. They may also feel angry. Some women describe this sort of barrage as psychological rape. Women fear the sexual harassment could escalate and/or they could lose their jobs. Unfortunately, neither of these is that unrealistic. Because women are often in lower grades in employment it can be difficult to complain about sexual harassment by men who are in more powerful positions, like their bosses. Male domination and workplace hierarchies can work together against a woman. Sexual harassment may be trivialised as 'harmless fun', assumed to be desirable flattery or seen to be a private matter. But sexual harassment is a serious violation of a woman.

When a woman is sexually harassed she is made to feel that she is no longer a worker but has become a sexual object. There is a loss of control over her identity as a worker and an individual women. This effects a woman's self-confidence and performance in employment. Instead of being valued for what she can accomplish, suddenly her value is as a sexual stereotype. There are two kinds of stereotypes commonly used against sexually harassed women. There is the 'bad sport' stereotype which is based on the assumption that sexual harassment is just 'typical men's behaviour', which women should play along with. This is when they use the old line that women just don't have a sense of humour. Or the 'whore' stereotype which assumes that working women are either 'available' to the men they work with, that they have somehow 'asked for it' or that women 'sleep their way to the top'.

Sexual harassment prevents equal opportunities. It is all about power. Not only does sexual harassment undermine women workers, but it has been used as a tactic against women who have demanded equal pay and those working in traditionally 'men's jobs'.

Strategies against sexual harassment

Individual women develop protective techniques against sexual harassment like avoidance (which can be difficult if the harasser works nearby) and changing their dress and behaviour to be more distant. When facing sexual harassment, without the support of others, many women quit or are fired, although some successfully stop the behaviour.

When women stand together they can be stronger. Because sexual harassment is about power relationships not 'harmless sexual fun', women find that by acting together they can have more power. In some cases women have found it necessary to turn the tables to demonstrate this. In one workplace there were many offensive pin-ups of women. The women workers asked to have them taken down, but were ignored. So they put up male pin-ups and the management quickly demanded that all pin-ups be removed.

Laws and unions

Too often sexual harassment has been seen as the problem of an individual woman who is suffering from it, but the reverse is true. It is the problem of male-dominated society and an economic system which puts profits above people. Attitudes, expectations and power relationships must be changed. In other words, sexual harassment reflects male power and the profit motive. Women shouldn't have to put up with it!

Some legal means have come into force against sexual harassment. In 1991 the European Commission adopted a code of practice which defined sexual harassment as, 'Unwanted conduct of a sexual nature, or other conduct based on sex, affecting the dignity of women and men at work'. It called on member states to promote awareness that sexual harassment was unacceptable and, although it is not binding, member states must take the code of practice into account in interpreting their own laws. In Britain a court decision in 1986 made sexual harassment illegal under the Sex Discrimination Act. In 1993 the European Court forced the British Government to remove the ceiling on damages both in sex and race discrimination cases.

In the US, guidelines were set up and government institutions and those getting federal funding had to establish complaint procedures for sexual harassment. There have also been private lawsuits. The issue gained national coverage when women complained of sexual harassment during hearings to appoint a supreme court judge.

In Britain some trade unions have played a role in fighting sexual harassment, although women have also had to fight against harassment by male union members and within unions. Women trade unionists have shown how sexual harassment is a union issue. It has not only been taken up by the Trades Union Council's Women's Conference but by the whole TUC itself, which drew up guidelines against sexual harassment. Trade unionists have taken up the issue of sexual harassment through women's discussion groups; branch meetings and workplace meetings structured by a film about sexual harassment; arguing against sexist jokes, comments and pictures; and bulletins and questionnaires. They have also focused on management polices and the use of sexist advertising by companies.

A number of different organisations have used questionnaires and surveys to raise consciousness and show the extent of the problem. This has also demonstrated that Black women have faced racial harassment which, at times, has been combined with sexual harassment.

Women in developing countries

Many women workers in **developing countries** (i.e. nations which are building up from their relatively low industrial capability and economic productivity) are even more exploited than women in Western industrialised nations. To understand how this has happened it is important to take a brief look at world economics. Historically, most developing countries were colonised, which meant they lost their economic independence to the colonising power. More recently there has been a world economic crisis. As Frances Stewart points out, the steady progress made in human conditions in the 1950s, 1960s and early 1970s in developing countries were tragically reversed in the 1980s; not mainly because of internal policies in developing countries but because of the world economic crisis.

The world economic crisis is complex. Put simply it started in the 1970s with Western banks encouraging developing countries to take out loans at what were then reasonable interest rates. The oil price rises in 1978–79 triggered a major world recession. This not only hurt industrialised countries but, in turn, depressed markets in developing nations, so that they could not sell their products. A major fall in commodity prices meant developing nations had to pay more for imports, but got paid less for the things they exported. Next came the rise of protectionism by industrialised nations, which cost developing nations more than the international aid they received. All of this meant that developing nations could neither earn what they needed nor easily borrow money. Their positive economic inflow in 1979 was transformed by 1986 to a negative outflow – that became the 'debt crisis'. As interest rates rose, lending opportunities dried up and development aid stagnated; many developing countries found they were paying out more to the industrialised world to service their loans than they were receiving in new aid and loans.

Developing countries were forced to use the only lender left to them, which was the International Monetary Fund, but they demanded cutbacks in social programmes in exchange for credit. These 'adjustment policies' translated into great suffering for the poorest people, a large portion of whom were women. Adjustment policies have meant that more women have gone into waged employment, working for low pay in extremely poor conditions, while some of the most skilled women in developing nations have had to leave their countries to look for employment.

Even with some women in more recognised employment, published data can make it look as if most women don't play a role in the economy of developing nations. This is not a true picture. It's just that their labour is not being counted. Beyond the domestic work of women, which is also uncounted in Western industrialised nations, women in developing nations are often small traders of goods and services or agricultural workers. For example, in Africa three-quarters of agricultural work is done by women. But in the West farming is seen from a male point of view. This means that although women grow half the world's food, most agricultural advisors are men who talk to other men. Especially in Africa, many women lost their traditional rights to the land they work through colonial laws and development policies which tend to only give out land to men.

Women's actions for better lives
Women in both developing and industrialised nations have become involved in actions to lift the ever-increasing burden on women in the developing world. In the West, women have worked to raise awareness of the unfair debt burden of developing nations which in 1986 meant that 30 billion US dollars was transferred from developing nations to industrialised countries. This money was taken out of the developing world while 40,000 children died each day and 800 million people lived in dire poverty.

In developing nations women have been involved in self-help projects, educational networks and cultural support projects. Research on and documentation of development issues has been done by The African Women's Communication and Development Network. In Kenya women are involved with action-oriented research and training, while in Ghana a Women's Credit Union has been set up. Women's World Banking has nearly a hundred locally organised and run groups to enable women to gain skills and capital. Feminist networks in Latin American countries like Chile, Argentina, Peru, the Dominican Republic and Brazil have set up communication strategies with poor women. The international women's network, Development Alternatives with Women for a New Era, is providing women's groups with research information for an analysis of the problems they face.

As Krishna Ahooja-Patel points out in her introduction to *Women and the World Economic Crisis*, when the world economic crisis is looked at from at women's viewpoint it is clear that one of the reasons that it continues is because women are kept from making decisions on national and international levels. She suggests that a number of aspects of the problem could be overcome if women were truly part of the solution.

Women workers organise
In *Dignity and Daily Bread*, Sheila Rowbotham and Swasti Mitter point out that changes in employment (discussed earlier in this chapter in the industrialised world) also effect the developing world, where women have used various strategies to gain more control of their working lives. In India the self-employed Women's Association is a union which organises different kinds of women workers including homeworkers, street vendors and contract workers. The Women's Association uses both union and co-operative methods to bargain for materials and resources which women need. The co-operative not only acts as a defence for poor women workers, but also provides an economic model involving women's democratic participation. In Mexico the Nineteenth of September Union of women garment workers not only organises around specific workplace conditions, but also around social needs. For example, it has started crèches.

Positive roles of women

Working-class feminism

As Heather Jon Maroney points out, working-class feminism is an important current within the women's movement in Western industrial countries like Canada. It has its roots in the workplace and focuses on issues like equal pay, training, women moving into traditional 'men's jobs', child care and sexual harassment. Working-class feminists tend to be active in unions and/or working-class communities. They may organise in their community, on their jobs within existing unions, or help women become unionised.

In Canada, particularly British Columbia, one strategy for organising non-unionised women was the feminist–syndicalist approach. The **feminist–syndicalist approach** to union organising involves building independent, women-controlled unions within industries which were mostly female and not unionised. An example of this approach was the Service, Office and Retail Workers Union of Canada (SORWUC), formed in 1972. Their early successes were based on using democratic, non-hierarchical models (including small consciousness-raising groups) and focusing on the issues which were most important to women. This not only helped women gain more power, it also demonstrated to what was called 'malestream' trade unions that women clerical and service workers could be organised. Heather Jon Maroney points out that as time went on the limitations of this approach became clearer, as SORWUC was isolated by its reaction against 'big' unionism and opposition to the Canadian Labour Congress. But the message that working-class women must have a political base to fight for their needs did get out to both the traditional labour movement and the feminist movement as a whole.

Non-unionised women have often been organised into existing unions to gain better pay and conditions. The Fleck strike, in Ontario, Canada in 1978, was an example of this. As the strike went on for months, trade union feminists mobilised women for picket lines and got financial support both from union women's committees and the feminist movement as a whole. This brought a feminist content to the strike and showed the value of the women's movement to the strikers and other unionists. It also gave non-union feminists a greater understanding of class issues. At the same time, the UAW parent union supported the Fleck women strikers by taking up collections of money and bringing in predominately male workers for mass picketing.

There was a coming together of class and gender solidarity. The Fleck women strikers felt that although management and the police thought they'd be more easily intimidated because they were women, instead they were able to hold out longer than men because they had solidarity as women. Maroney sees working-class and socialist feminists as bringing an important class conscious current into the women's movement as a whole.

Working-class women have played a leading role in defending their communities, as they did in the 1984/85 miners strike in Britain. They demonstrated their ability to speak, write, organise and picket to defend their mining communities. The male strikers came to respect and depend on women supporters in groups such as Women Against Pit Closures. Women did a variety of tasks, some of which moved them beyond their traditional roles, demonstrating their potential not only to the miners and their own children but to themselves and the labour movement generally.

A history of strikes and actions to gain equality

Historically, as today, women have organised and fought for improvements in their working lives. (See Chapter 2 for some specific examples.) In Britain much legislation has come about as a response to women's struggles at work. I have already mentioned one example: in 1968 women at the Dagenham motor plant struck for recognition of their skills and shut down the whole plant. Their actions led to the promise of equal pay legislation and a large demonstration by women for equal pay in Trafalgar Square in 1969. Of course, women had been demonstrating for equal pay long before that. And since then women have organised many strikes for their rights. In 1982, for example, Asian women textile workers struck for 12 weeks at Smethwick, West Midlands, for union recognition and better pay. Black women have played a leading role in many actions for union recognition.

Women in trade unions

Historically, women organised unions for women, as well as being active in mixed sex unions. Although, at times, unions have helped to exclude women from particular jobs and discouraged women's participation, they have also played an important role in improving women's working lives. Women in employment have often seen that they gain protection and pay increases by being in a union.

Today, some unions are more conscious of the problems of part-time women workers and have actively tried to deal with them. Female trade unionists have pushed for greater participation of women at all levels of the union structure and some women are now in leadership roles. A number of trade unions have seen the importance of female role models in organising women. Although some women have now been encouraged to be more active, lack of child care and traditional sexist attitudes still stand in their way.

In Britain the TUC has organised courses to encourage women's participation in unions. Although things have changed from the days when some women got whistled at and had remarks made about their appearance when they got up to speak at conferences, there are still changes necessary. Women have pointed out that men don't necessarily understand their problems, as many have different jobs and lifestyles. Because so many women have domestic responsibilities it is especially difficult to balance all the demands on their time when they are active in the union. Positive actions taken by some unions include child care at all meetings or a child care allowance, women's committees, women's officers and reserved seats for women on union committees.

Some working-class and socialist feminists have argued that through women joining unions and becoming active in them they will gain more protection, job security, control over their jobs and higher pay. They will also be able to raise issues which are important to women. A number of working-class women have gained skills and confidence through union participation, which has enabled them to go on to leadership roles, better jobs and higher levels of education.

A personal note

As a member of two unions, The Writers Guild of Great Britain and the University and College Lecturers' Union, NATFHE, I have seen both the problems in unions and the power and protection they can offer. Certainly they are not perfect, but I know that I have personally gained by being in them. It is just too easy to be blown over, standing alone against the corporate winds. Not only have I been represented by unions in difficult situations, but I've also been able to use them as a vehicle to bring up feminist issues for discussion and action. Being on the Women's Committee of the Writers Guild has been a particularly good way to do this.

Understanding our differences and coming together

Equal pay and child care were two of the original demands of the Women's Liberation Movement, which was predominately middle class. A number of working-class feminists have criticised the women's movement for ignoring the concerns of working-class women. More recently there's been an effort to acknowledge and understand our class differences. Although many middle-class women work part time under difficult conditions, it is working-class women who bear the brunt of low pay and the worst working conditions. Yet women in employment have common problems like job segregation by gender, sexual harassment and child care. It is important to be clear about the exploitation of working-class women and their communities, while understanding what unites women and how we can join together to create better lives.

Employment can bring women together who might otherwise not have met one another and can give them common ground on which to unite. If we network with other women across occupations, classes, races, levels of abilities and sexual orientations we can broaden ourselves and gain needed support. Because women in paid work have a number of common problems there is room to form alliances to create a stronger force for better conditions. This includes uniting beyond national boundaries.

At the time of writing this (March 1996) there is an interesting example of people coming together around common employment problems in the state of California in the US. One way in which the US has tried to make up for past discrimination against groups such as women and people of colour (like African Americans, Asian Americans, Latinos and Native Americans) is through affirmative action programmes. **Affirmative action** programmes increase opportunities for members of under represented groups in areas like employment. There is now an anti-affirmative action initiative on the ballot in California and pressure nationally to end it. This has brought feminist groups like the National Organisation of Women into an alliance with the Coalition of Color, labour organisations and lesbians and gays. They have come together, trying to transcend identity politics, to create a movement to save affirmative action and struggle against the right-wing ideas behind the move to end it.

Breaking through the glass ceiling

Women are held back by the glass ceiling in many areas where their input might help to change the expectations and treatment of women. They have campaigned, created networks, used legal channels and individually persisted in order to break the glass ceiling. A number of feminists have pointed out the importance of women, who come into positions of power, not taking on the values and characteristic ways of behaving of male-dominated society. Clearly, it is not easy to make one's way in a profit-oriented, male-dominated society and still maintain a vision of one's self as a woman who wants a just society.

In March 1996 I attended a meeting of women in the media. Although a number of the women there were writing, producing or directing for radio, television or theatre there was a clear feeling that women still needed to break through the glass ceiling to more powerful positions in the male-dominated media. Too often men were looking for people like themselves to hire. In broadcasting journalism where some positions for women were tokenistic, single women without children were sometimes not hired because men said they did not represent most women, while those who had a second child sometimes didn't have their contracts renewed because men thought it was too much of a strain for them. A number of women who had been discriminated against felt they couldn't institute legal actions because they'd never get another job in the industry. Some women expressed concern about the backlash which had taken place in the last five years. Others discussed the enormous strain, after they had had children, to prove that they could still work all the hours considered necessary.

There were positive advancements discussed where a number of women who had gained more powerful positions consciously encouraged other women and challenged stereotyped portrayals of women in the media. Some women had campaigned for governing boards to be made up of 50 per cent women.

Hope for future generations

Both in and out of the home, women have struggled to gain power over their working lives. Although there are still barriers, there is also a determination to overcome them and the hope that future generations of women will grow up with more opportunities and less limiting expectations. An example of wider expectations is presented by Heidi Mirza in *Young, Female and Black*. She shows evidence that both second-generation West Indian young women in Britain and young Black women in the West Indies did not see any difference between their ability to work and the kind of work they could do and that of men. Black girls were more likely to say they wanted to do non-gendered work than white girls. Mirza sees this sexual equality concerning work as stemming from the external oppression of Black societies. Many young Black women had not taken on dominant Eurocentric gender ideas, instead their definition of male and female capabilities at work had few distinctions.

EXERCISE 8.5 Finding your dream job

1 What is your dream job? Sit comfortably in a quiet room and close your eyes. Take a few deep breaths and try to relax. Now let yourself image your dream job. Don't worry about the fact that it might not seem practical or possible for you to do it. Just visualise yourself doing the kind of job that you want to do.

2 How can you begin to move toward getting your dream job? (First, you'll need to believe it's possible.) What kind of skills would you need to develop?

3 Make a plan of what you'd need to do to get your dream job. Try taking the first step on the plan. Then move on to the next one.

9

INTO THE
TWENTY-FIRST
CENTURY

Sparked by the idealism of making a better world, we came to believe that we could create change for women; even if we couldn't see exactly what those changes would bring. As we move into the twenty-first century the struggle for further changes may take different forms. Beyond the present, often defensive, posture we need to have a vision for the future and to remember the power of change. For it is through that process that we transform ourselves.

Acknowledging our successes

In order to look towards a future of empowerment and to believe in our ability to create the necessary changes to make that happen, both in society and in our own lives, it can be useful to acknowledge some of the changes which women have been able to bring about this century. In many countries women gained the right to vote and other legal rights. More women went to schools and universities and entered jobs and professions from which they had been barred. This potentially enabled them to have more confidence, power and independence. Some women gained control of their fertility through the use of birth control and abortion. Women forced society to at least begin to be more conscious of attitudes toward females and expectations of them, as well as taking violence against women more seriously. These have been truly great victories, which women have struggled for and won. And they have changed the lives of many women.

Over the last 25 years, with the second wave of feminism, I have personally witnessed enormous changes in women's lives brought about by our individual and collective efforts. They range from women having taken more control of their sexuality to having gained a wider range of employment, and from words and concepts like sexism and sexual harassment coming into the vocabulary (and to some extent cultural consciousness) to women gaining more legal and financial independence. Of course, these are only partial victories, which vary in different countries, but they are powerful successes none the less.

Recently I helped to organise a reunion of the London Chalk Farm Women's Consciousness Raising Group which I attended in 1970 and 1971. Coming back together after all those years, we were reminded of the supportive atmosphere and idealism of the group, as well as the non-hierarchical dynamic where women came to listen intently to one another as much as to speak. It was a wonderful evening full of richness and laughter (sometimes at ourselves back then) in which it became clear that we had all been deeply affected by being a part of that moment in women's history. The consciousness raising group had helped us to gain power and independence as well as a deeper understanding of ourselves as women. We had all come to internalise a feminist consciousness and this had changed our lives – from the woman who has become a feminist therapist to the housewife and mother organising at her local women's centre and from the occupational health adviser to the co-operative housing development worker.

A new generation of women have now come of age with their own perspectives and agendas. Beatrix Campbell says they are 'raunchier, ruder, braver and better balanced ... and their commitment to feminist issues is palpable'. (*Guardian* 11 May 1995). Kate Figes points out in *Because of her Sex* that even women who have grown up without realising that they have been influenced by feminism have taken on heightened expectations. She believes this is so even though feminism has done much more to highlight discrimination than to change it; but feminism has stirred up debate, challenging traditional attitudes and making its way into the souls of young women, even though they may not want to call themselves feminists. Clearly, the point for some young women is not the title, but the changes in attitudes which they have adopted. This often involves issues such as young women valuing their independence and wanting to continue to have financial independence even if they decide to have children. Sheila Rowbotham brings in another perspective when she makes the point that 'the women's movement is created by new generations in different ways. Now it's being recreated by women in the Third World' (*Guardian* 11 May 1995).

Acknowledging our oppression

As well as looking at our victories it is also useful to understand the oppression we face.

External oppression

Throughout this book I have discussed numerous ways in which women are oppressed. Here are some worldwide statistics from Oxfam to put this in perspective.

- Two-thirds of illiterate people are women.
- One-third of households are headed by women.
- Women typically earn 30–40 per cent less than men for the same jobs.
- Every minute one woman dies of causes related to pregnancy and childbirth.
- One woman in every 2,000 has been reported as raped and large numbers of women don't report being raped.
- Women and children make up 80 per cent of refugees and displaced people.
- There were only six women who were heads of governments in 1993.
- Only 1.4 per cent of television news items deal with women's issues and three-quarters of these are presented by men.

Internalising society's expectations and values

Too often we have internalised society's expectations and they stand within us like a guard, limiting both how we perceive and think about the world and what we can accomplish. Rather than consciously deciding to take on certain tasks, such as tidying up after others, we may automatically do them because we and those around us expect that this is our role. In order to move beyond internalised limitations, so that we can make more conscious choices, it may be helpful to be clear about exactly what internalised expectations are and how we have been affected and defined by them.

EXERCISE 9.1 **Looking at our internalised expectations**

1 Put a check mark next to any of the following statements that you generally expect yourself to do.

A Give your time and energies to others at the expense of having enough for yourself.

B Set the needs of others as a high priority and your own needs as a low priority.

C Have men take the lead, while you help them.

D Believe that you are not able to take an active role.

E Believe that men are more intelligent.

F Believe that men should be more powerful and authoritative.

2 Look at any statement which you have marked. Is it helpful to you to have this expectation? Can you describe any ways in which it is not helpful? Would you like to modify the expectation or change it completely?

3 Can you think of any other internalised expectations which you would like to change? – for example, expectations about your own value and capabilities.

4 How have you been affected and defined by your internalised expectations? How has this limited you? What effects would it have on you if you could change your internalised expectations?

Nurturing ourselves

Looking at our internalised expectations can be the start of a very freeing process, opening up wider possibilities. It involves discovering more about how we see ourselves and our identity. This may also be a difficult process, bring up pain and vulnerability. In coming to terms with this it may be helpful to remember that women are often skilled at nurturing other people, but we can nurture ourselves, as well. I remember my sister telling me that after she had a baby she found she had no time or energy left for herself, until she came to see that she also had to be her own mother. Women are often expected to value others above themselves. However, by nurturing and developing ourselves we may not only be happier and stronger, but have more positive energies to share with others.

Moving towards empowerment

Although it is not an easy thing for women (individually or in groups) to move beyond society's limiting expectations and values to gain power, women have made and can make changes in society and in themselves. There can be an enormous sense of freedom in moving beyond male-dominated expectations and having more control of our lives and values. This can give us the opportunity to envision and theorise about fairer ways for women all over the world to live, as well as to discuss individual and group strategies toward this empowerment. In a time when many women find themselves in a defensive position – between the world economic crisis, the ever-present pressures of male-dominated values and the so-called 'backlash' – this ability to conceive of ways forward is especially important.

Individual strategies

Believing in ourselves
Women are not highly valued in male-dominated society. This, combined with other factors, may make it more difficult for women to believe in themselves. Recognising society's expectations may be helpful in the process of building confidence, because it shows that women's undervaluing of themselves is not an individual problem and that each woman who lacks confidence is not alone. Just as society's values can change, our own internalised expectations can also be affected, although often this is not easy. It can be helpful to develop more positive feelings about ourselves.

Not being governed by society's expectations
Our internalised expectations are part of a complex process in which, at times, there are competing and even opposing expectations on different levels. Still, becoming aware of at least some of the expectations which we have internalised may be helpful in developing strategies to be more conscious of them and their implications and act accordingly.

I sometimes think of these internalised expectations as tape recordings which run in my mind. I may not be able to stop the tape from running, but that doesn't mean I have to do what it says or agree with it. For example, I have caught myself thinking that the

EXERCISE 9.2 **Developing kindness toward ourselves**

1 Sit or lie comfortably in a room by yourself.
2 Follow the relaxation instructions in Exercise 5.6 number 2.
3 Create the positive visualisation suggested in the first two paragraphs of Exercise 5.6 number 3. Continue the visualisation as follows.
4 Image a good friend, whom you can trust, coming toward you in your peaceful, enchanted place. As she moves closer you see she is radiant, smiling at you. She joins you and there is a warm glow in the air.

She tells you of her good news, which she truly deserves. Allow yourself to feel pleased for her. Savour this special moment which you share together. Giving her your good wishes she returns the same, wishing you well. Take a few minutes to enjoy the sending and receiving of this kindness.

As your friend prepares to leave she advises you, 'Give yourself those same good wishes which you were sending to me. Whatever has happened you deserve your own loving kindness.'

Allow yourself to feel your own good wishes. Savour the glow of kindness within you as you nurture yourself. Perhaps you can image a warmth in the centre of your chest which emanates outward filling your whole body with your own gentle love. Take a few minutes to focus on this kindness for yourself.

As you build up the light of loving kindness for yourself, you can radiate it outward toward others.
5 When you are ready to finish the session, do so slowly. Take a moment to return to thinking about your body. Feel yourself back in the room where you are sitting or lying. Starting with your feet, allow a feeling of awakening to work its way through your body. Stretch and then open your eyes.
6 You can return to your special place whenever you like to develop loving kindness toward yourself and others. You might try reading this visualisation into a tape recorder, including pauses, so that you can listen to it and more easily take part in the visualisation.

If you feel emotional pain try giving yourself loving kindness; nurture yourself without either forcing the pain away or feeding into it. Try acknowledging how you feel and being kind to yourself.

work which women do is not as important as what men do. I've come to understand that there's no point in being angry at myself for this, as it's clearly an internalised expectation of society's values. Besides, if I were to get angry at myself I wouldn't want to consciously catch myself next time an internalised expectation tape ran through my brain. Instead, I think, 'Good I've caught that one. That's good, now I can act accordingly.' I try to be conscious not to use the expectation as the basis for my actions or decisions. I ask myself what a truer understanding of the situation would be. After I've been through this a few times with a particular expectation I find that just becoming conscious of it running through my mind is enough to take the power out of it and after a while it tends to come to mind less often.

EXERCISE 9.3 **Becoming conscious of internalised expectations**

1 Think about any internalised expectations which you tend to have. Do you ever remember hearing them running through your mind? If so, what effect does this tend to have on you?

2 Make a list of your internalised expectations. Be positive toward yourself each time you discover another one, rather than being annoyed that you could possibly think that.

3 For each internalised expectation which you have discovered, think of a more accurate view and write it down.

4 Try to be conscious of your internalised expectations as you move through your daily life. Be positive toward yourself each time you discover one and think of a more accurate view.

Redefining ourselves

Because women have so often been defined in limiting ways by society, it may be helpful to think of how you want to define yourself. Try to create a definition which is both positive and empowering. You may want to expand Exercise 5.7 (Self-praise and affirmations) to create more general affirmations about yourself and use them in your own empowering definition.

Groups

Many women have found that through being involved in groups with other women they have been individually empowered as well as helping to gain more collective power. Not only can group participation break through a sense of isolation, but it demonstrates how women can create changes in society by working together. See the appendix for contact addresses of various groups.

Women's groups
The women's movement has taken many different forms, working for change in various areas. Women throughout the world have come together based on their needs and special interests to form organisations such as action groups, information networks and alternative women's media groups. In Britain, for example, this includes groups from Women's Aid Federation to Women in Publishing and from the Working Mothers Association to the Asian Young Women's Project. In many countries there have been feminist demonstrations and meetings, community action campaigns, various forms of women's centres, refuges, telephone help lines and women's co-operatives.

Women's involvement in various movements for justice
In many parts of the world women have played an important role in movements for justice such as workers' movements, peace movements and movements for the rights of ethnic minorities. They have either formed their own organisations such as the Women's International League for Peace and Freedom, formed caucuses such as women's sections in trade unions or worked within broader movements such as civil groups.

Women's involvement in other forms of politics
Through suffrage movements in many parts of the world women gained the vote and some women began to play a role in government. Although women have often been limited in their participation in government, there have been some improvements and a number of women politicians believe they can make a difference if enough women become involved in this form of public life. (Drude Dahlerup, a political science lecturer in Denmark, has demonstrated that quotas for women is an efficient way to increase their political representation.) Women have formed their own political organisations, such as the Three Hundred Group in Britain which is working for an equal number of women and men in parliament. They

have also formed political caucuses and lobbies for a women's agenda in politics.

Women have played an important role in struggles for national liberation such as in Algeria, China, Eritrea, Namibia, Nicaragua, Mozambique, Palestine, Vietnam and Zimbabwe. In South Africa, the Philippines and many parts of Latin America they have played a significant role in movements for greater democracy. In South Africa, the Women's National Coalition has been formed (made up of Black and white women from 60 different organisations) to ensure that the laws and the constitution guarantee women's rights. The African National Congress Women's League was successful in ensuring that the ANC adopted a policy of having one-third of their candidates in the 1994 election be women.

Feminists tend to define politics broadly, seeing the personal as political. In this way, women's involvement in many different activities are considered political. For example, women have often organised demonstrations which have had a strong political effect. They have organised strikes and other actions for women's rights, as discussed earlier in this book.

Women in international organisations

As Marilee Karl points out in *Women and Empowerment*, when the United Nations (UN) was formed in 1945 women from national and international organisations helped to create the support necessary to include the principle of equal rights of women and men in the UN Charter. In 1946, the Commission on the Status of Women (CSW) was established to prepare reports and recommendations on women's political, economic, civil, social and educational rights. The Secretariat for the CSW is the Division for the Advancement of Women, (located in New York) which is the main unit within the UN dealing with women. It is a contact point for women with an information and research centre.

Since the 1970s women have been more active in and around the UN. The International Women's Year (1975), the Decade for Women (1976–85) and the Beijing Women's Conference (1995) were UN landmarks and rallying points for mobilising women internationally.

The UN Beijing Women's Conference and the NGO Forum

As Susana Fried of the Centre for Women's Global Leadership points out, the theme of the Beijing UN Women's Conference was that women's rights are human rights. At the Non-governmental Organisation (NGO) Forum, which took place at the same time, there was a women's human rights caucus which lobbied governmental delegates for human rights issues to be included throughout the Platform for Action (the official document to be agreed upon by the 189 countries at the conference).

The Platform for Action dealt with *some* of women's basic human rights including outlawing use of sexual violence, government promotion of women's rights and non-discrimination laws, literacy, as well as global peace, refugees, and development of women's leadership skills.

In the end, the Platform showed concern for individual women's rights, rather than collective rights involving women's economic position. Although the Platform sets out broad parameters, it contains few references to economic, cultural and social rights. While the women's human rights caucus did not get all their recommendations into the Platform, it does use strong language to commit governments to protect and promote women's human rights in new areas. Susana Fried believes that in the long run how helpful the Platform will be to women depends on how much they are able to use it to promote policies and actions for women's rights.

Critics of the Platform believe that it does not make the necessary links between current economic models and women's lack of empowerment; Beijing did not challenge the international financial institutions which have the power to set both economic agendas and the terms of debates concerning women's equality. Critics believe this is because international financial institutions are the main lenders for development funding, making governments and their women's ministries beholden to them; this holds back women's movements and justifies free-market prescriptions which demand cuts in social programmes desperately needed by poor women.

Helen O'Connell sees the issue of economic justice as the main focus of follow-up work after the conference, as women are determined that their economic rights should be recognised. She says that because 'resources, wealth and technology are monopolised by a powerful few, marginalising the majority' there are two main challenges. First, reducing poverty and redistributing wealth and resources so that extremely poor women receive a fair share. Second, making the world economy more democratic. (*links* February 1996)

International women's activities

Women have been involved in non-governmental international activities such as demonstrations at embassies, petition and letter campaigns and collections of money. For example, Lidia Falcón describes how when the Feminist Party was struggling to be legalised in Spain (from 1979 to 1981) telegrams and letters from women in many different parts of the world were instrumental in helping them achieve their goal. In *Sisterhood is Global*, Robin Morgan suggests that actions such as demonstrations could be internationally co-ordinated through growing feminist networks. For example, she suggests women in various countries add one another's specific demands to their own in demonstrations which are held on the same day in many countries.

Regional and international networking has been useful. Examples of this can be seen in Latin American history. In 1910, the First

International Feminist Congress was held in Argentina and the Pan-American Feminist Federation was organised in Chile. At the present time, Women's Aid to former Yugoslavia has been organising convoys of humanitarian aid in Britain and delivering the aid to women's organisations of all ethnic groups.

Education

One important way for women to gain more power is through education. This is useful on various levels from literacy to university education. Beyond learning to read and write, as this book has demonstrated, the ability of women to reclaim and theorise about female experiences is an essential part of their empowerment. Education is necessary for many forms of participation and communication, without which women find themselves restricted.

There are 600 million illiterate women in the world (over twice as many as men). They tend to be employed in lower-paying jobs and to be less productive than educated women. They marry younger and are less likely to use family planning, to be able to keep their children healthy or send them to school. Although it is important to remember that education alone does not bring equality and that literacy is neither a sign of intelligence nor necessary for wisdom; the education of illiterate women is a primary demand in order for them and their children to gain power over their lives and a decent standard of living. It is also necessary for an ecologically sound, fairer world, as women are better able to protect their environment, be productive and share in prosperity if they are educated.

Women's studies

In this book I have only been able to offer you a taste of the subject of women's studies. There are whole areas which I haven't even touched upon. For example; the hidden history of women artists, their undisplayed works of art and the present struggle of women artists. There has been some progress on this front such as the establishment of the National Museum of Women in the Arts in Washington, DC, in the US. The museum celebrates and makes known the achievements of present and past women artists.

Now that you've had a taste of women's studies, why not consider taking a course? This would give you an opportunity to explore your specific interests, meet other women and generally develop your

[margin note: importance of education for empowerment.]

knowledge to help you obtain your goals. Women's studies courses are taught in many countries on a variety of levels. These include pre-university, undergraduate and graduate courses. For example, in Britain, the wide variety of courses include those taught by the Workers' Educational Association (WEA), women's centres, community colleges, further education colleges and large numbers of universities throughout the country (including an excellent course taught through the Open University). Women's studies can be a primary area of study up to a PhD or it can be a module, paper or course in a programme of study. Feminist research, critiques and approaches have also become a part of many other areas of study. See the appendix for contact listings or consult your local women's centre, library, college or university.

Into the twenty-first century – imagining a just world

As we move into the twenty-first century, it could be useful to envision various possibilities for fairer expectations and values throughout the world based on feminist ideas. This would give us an opportunity to clarify our thoughts, set goals and work toward them.

EXERCISE 9.4 Your vision of fairer world values

1 How could feminist ideas help to create a fairer future?
2 Specifically which feminist values would you like to see adopted throughout the world? What effect would they have?
3 What would you envision a just world to be like in the twenty-first century?

There could be many possible visions for the future based on various understandings of feminism and different views about it.

For me, a just world would involve valuing women and having them play an equal role in a new society. Women's participation, based on co-operation and the notion of valuing people rather than profits, could bring an equitable worldwide prosperity. I envision a kind of democracy, where people have economic as well as political control of their lives. This would involve them making decisions on how they lived and worked themselves, on a local level, rather than top-down government and industrial management. Universal education, based on concern for and an understanding of the lives of all peoples and with the goal of assisting each girl and boy to learn to think for themselves, would assist in this process. Feminist values such as co-operation and concern for others (including future generations) would then make it possible for women in the leadership of fairly elected councils, whose representatives could easily be recalled if necessary, to work with local areas to co-ordinate decisions. Up through a worldwide level, power would be based on mass participation and the sharing of wealth.

Using feminist values the goals of technology would be to improve peaceful, co-operative living. The money now spent on instruments of distruction would be available to feed and house the poorest women and their families and to give them the resources they need to become self-sufficient. Technology is an example of how setting new ground rules, beyond a male-dominated vision of limited cause and effect, could widen possibilities for positive uses of science and machines involving broad-based control by people, with the goal of best serving them. This would turn around many of our present notions. For example, we are told that there are less jobs necessary because of technology. But if technology freed us from some forms of work, and if the goal was caring for people rather than profits, then the many necessary caring jobs which women often do for free or for low pay could be seriously undertaken. Jobs could be shared so that there would be enough work for everyone, shortening working hours.

As well as there being universal, high-quality child care, working in the home would be highly valued. The sharing of housework and child care would mean more time for everyone, which would benefit both children and adults. Not only would this be helpful for women, but it would also help men lead fuller more caring lives.

When women set a priority of valuing living beings rather than profits, the interrelationship with the environment becomes clear to sustain healthy living for all. It would be essential to work with and respect the environment, as women did during the era of goddess worship.

Violence against people would be considered the worst crime, but as future generations were raised in a nurturing, equitable environment such actions would greatly decrease.

Women and men would be free to express their sexuality in any ways which were not abusive. Women could choose their partners and their lifestyles to balance the broader context of concern for others with their own personal needs.

Although my vision seems utopian, I believe what could make it possible would be enormous changes in attitudes and values. With the rising dawn of the new century we hold the potential to transform our lives and the lives of the millions of poverty-stricken women throughout the world by valuing women, co-operating and more equitably sharing wealth so that we could all prosper.

APPENDIX – CONTACT LISTINGS

BRITAIN

Women's Studies Network
Centre for Research on Education and Gender
Institute of Education
University of London
20 Bedford Way
London WC1H 0AL
Tel: 0171 612 6245
Fax: 0171 612 6177

Fawcett Library
London Guildhall University
Old Castle Street
London E1 7NT
Tel: 0171 320 1189
Fax: 0171 320 1188

National Alliance of Women's Organisations
PO Box 257
Twickenham TW1 4XG
Tel: 0181 891 1419

Women's Aid Federation (Women's Refuges)
PO BOX 391
Bristol BS99 7WS
National Help Line
Tel: 0117 963 3542

Everywoman Directory of Women's Studies Courses and
Everywoman Directory of Women's Organisations
Everywoman Magazine
9 St Alban's Place
London N1 0NX
Tel: 0171 359 5496

UNITED STATES

National Women's Studies Association
University of Maryland
College Park, Maryland 20742
Tel: (301) 403-0525
e-mail: priya@info.umd.edu

National Organization for Women
1000 16th Street NW
Washington DC
Tel: (202) 331-0066

Schlesinger Library
Radcliff College
10 Garden Street
Cambridge, Mass. 02138
Tel: (617) 495-8647
Fax: (617) 496-8340

AUSTRALIA

The Australian Institute for Women's Research and Policy
Nathan Campus of Griffith University
4111 Queensland
Tel: (07) 3875 6582
Fax: (07) 3875 5333
e-mail: A.Corrigan@hum.gu.edu.au

The Jessie Street Women's Library
GPO Box 2656
Sidney, New South Wales 2001
Tel: (02) 5559376

CONTINENTAL EUROPE

Women's International Studies Europe
Heidelberglaan 2
3584 CS
Utrecht, Netherlands
Tel: (030) 2531881

International Information Centre and Archive for the Women's
  Movement (IIAV)
Obiplein 4
1094 RB
Amsterdam, Netherlands
Tel: (020) 6650820
Fax: (020) 6655812

CANADA

Canadian Women's Studies Association
University of Ottawa
550 Cumberland
Ottawa, Ontario
K1N 6N5
Tel: (613) 233-4929

FURTHER READING

Books on women's history and contemporary life

Bryan, B. *et al.*, *The Heart Of The Race – Black Women's Lives In Britain* (Virago 1985)

Holdsworth, A., *Out Of The Dolls House* (BBC Books 1988)

Karl, M., *Women And Empowerment – Participation and Decision Making* (Zed 1995)

Keith, L. (ed.), *Mustn't Grumble – Writing By Disabled Women* (Women's Press 1994)

Lesbian History Group, *Not a Passing Phase – Reclaiming Lesbians in History* (Women's Press 1989)

Miles, R., *The Women's History Of The World* (Michael Joseph 1988)

Rowbotham, S., *Women In Movement – Feminism And Social Action* (Routledge 1993)

Books which survey various topics in women's studies

Bonner, F. *et al.* (ed.) *Imagining Women – Cultural Representations and Gender* (Polity Press 1992)

Crowley, H. *et al.* (ed.), *Knowing Women – Feminism and Knowledge* (Polity Press 1992)

Humm, M. (ed.), *Feminisms – A Reader* (Harvester Wheatsheaf 1992)

Jackson, S. *et al.* (ed.), *Women's Studies – A Reader* (Harvester Wheatsheaf 1993)

McDowell, L. *et al.* (ed.), *Defining Women – Social Institutions and Gender Divisions* (Polity Press 1992)

Richardson, D. *et al.* (ed.), *Introducing Women's Studies* (Macmillan 1993)

Books on women's writing
Humm, M., *Border Traffic – Strategies of Contemporary Women Writers* (Manchester University Press 1991)

Showalter, E., *A Literature Of Their Own* (Virago 1995 – latest publisher)

Books on women's bodies and minds
Phillips, A. *et al.*, *New Our Bodies, Ourselves – A Health Book For And By Women* (Penguin 1996)

Stanko, E., *Intimate Intrusions – Women's Experience Of Male Violence* (Routledge & Kegan Paul 1985)

Walker, M., *Women In Therapy and Counselling* (Open University Press 1990)

INDEX